MODEL AIRPLANES

A MINIATURE HISTORY OF AVIATION

With an introduction by Toby Wrigley

CRESCENT BOOKS

Contents

All the photographs in this book were taken by Philip O. Stearns,
with the exception of the biplane on the cover and plate 5,
which are by Bill Hearne and plates 10–15, which are by Jan Lukas

The hobby of aeromodelling has grown with the development of the airplane itself to the fascinating and popular pastime that it is today. Flying models out of doors is as widespread as ever, but non-flying scale display models have been found to be better suited to the confines of the home, especially when storage becomes a problem. Shop-bought plastic kits, which enable anyone capable of assembling the parts to produce a realistic model, sell in their thousands. The most expert modellers, however, often regard kit models as the raw material for an intricate and beautiful job of conversion which will result in a unique model. And because a model of this sort does not look like a model, it was decided to make this book a history of the airplane, and to illustrate it with the best models available.

The publishers would like to express their thanks for the indefatigable research of Toby Wrigley and the brilliant photography of Philip O. Stearns, the collaborating authors of this book. They in turn wish to thank the many members of the International Plastic Modellers Society who have contributed to this book. These members include: Barrie Armstrong, W. R. Matthews, Norman Whitcomb and Harry Woodman, of London; J. R. Chisman, of Billericay; D. Warmington, of Birmingham; Tom and Michael Moore, of Bromley; K. Spackman and B. Owen, of Derby; Roger Chesneau, of Epping; A. M. L. Kennaugh, of Leamington Spa; J. Ellis, M. F. Harrop and D. Spicer, of Nottingham; Alan Butler, of Orpington; Donald and Finlay Skinner, of Oxford; Gordon Stevens and R. Rowley, of Redhill; Fred Henderson, of Woking; and Tony Woollett, of Wokingham. Special thanks are due to Paul E. Parker, of New York, for permission to photograph his unique collection of World War 1 models.

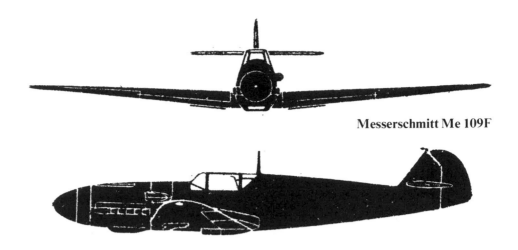

Messerschmitt Me 109F

The first flying machine

During the first years of the twentieth century, two brothers, bicycle manufacturers, were experimenting with man-lifting gliders among the sand dunes near Kitty Hawk, North Carolina. These experiments were to lead to the first successful heavier-than-air powered flying machine.

It seems amazing now that the success of these experiments on the 17th December, 1903, when Orville Wright made the first powered flight of 12 seconds, to be followed later that day by his brother with a flight of 59 seconds, did not hit the headlines of the world's newspapers. Locally, because of damage to the 'Flyer', it was looked on as another failure by two slightly mad enthusiasts.

By 1905 the brothers had a fully manoeuvrable airplane in their Flyer No III. They approached the US Army only to be told, to their amazement, that until a machine was produced capable of carrying a man in horizontal flight the War Department was not likely to be interested in their projects.

Wilbur then took a crated Flyer to France, but he did not even bother to assemble it because of the lack of interest. By 1908, however, knowledge of their success had reached other enthusiasts, and in the USA an official test was organized. In France the crated Flyer was assembled and on the 8th August, near Le Mans, Wilbur demonstrated the machine by flying in two graceful circuits with complete control, something of which no European machine was capable. This time the flight, and the subsequent longer ones, caused headlines throughout Europe. The arrival of the air age was hailed by newspapers everywhere.

For some months past European aeronauts had been achieving short hops in various primitive machines Santos Dumont and Voison had both built aircraft but neither had anything like the control and duration of the Wright Flyer. The Europeans were quick to learn, and the next year saw the appearance of many different designs – a sudden birth of so much that had been long gestating. Voison, Farman, A. V. Roe, Santos Dumont,

Blériot and Levavasseur all demonstrated successful machines, as did Glen Curtiss in the USA.

It was Blériot, on the 25th July, 1909, who flew the Channel across the Straits of Dover when 'England ceased to be an island'. This event caught the world's imagination as a portent for the future.

In August an aviation week was organized at Reims and here it was seen how much had been done in such a short time. Ten different types of airplane were on display and the Grand Prix was won by the 'French Englishman', Henri Farman, in his biplane, with a flight of three hours five minutes over a distance of 180 kms (about 112 miles).

Airplanes were becoming divided into two, or rather three, types: first, the pusher biplane with the engine behind the pilot, like the Wright machines; second, the tractor biplane such as the Avro; and third, tractor monoplanes such as the Blériot. Public interest still did not bring much Government support as military advisers were not greatly interested in the new 'toy'.

During the next year or two, however, embryo air services began to be formed by most major powers, often started by officers who had learnt to fly at their own expense. The French authorities purchased four machines in 1910 for the training of pilots; a German Air Service was already in being based on the Zeppelin. Italian, Russian and Austrian army officers all obtained their brevets in 1910. The US Army had already purchased a Wright Flyer in 1909 and the first fatality in powered aviation was a Lieutenant Thomas E. Selfridge, US Army, who was killed in a plane flown by Orville Wright. In Britain the order for creating an Air Battalion of the Royal Engineers was not issued until 1911, and the airplane had its first baptism of fire when it was used in the Balkan war of 1912.

By now it was obvious to many that the international situation was worsening, and the new air services in Britain had gained a strong advocate in the First Lord of the Admiralty, Mr Winston Churchill, who made several flights himself. More money was made available to constructors, and it was Government policy in several countries to see that there was an 'industry' built up to back the new services with machines and supplies.

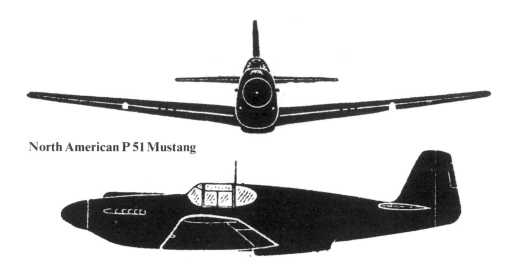

North American P 51 Mustang

The airplane goes to war

A few days after the British ultimatum to Germany
expired and the British Empire was at war, the four active
squadrons of the Royal Flying Corps – numbers 2 to 5 –
flew their machines across the Channel for the support of
the BEF. The rapid progress of aviation is shown in that
only five years after Blériot's flights in 1909, here were
some fifty airplanes in flight.

The machines that were in service at the outbreak of
the war were generally two-seaters capable of about
70 mph. There was no effort to equip them with weapons
for air fighting, though experiments with machine-guns
had been carried out in most services. The job of the
airplane, as seen by the generals, was to act as aerial
cavalry and gain information for the armies as they
manoeuvred. When the static war of the trenches took
over, however, a new pattern of aerial warfare developed.
The artillery observation balloons or aircraft were so
effective that they could not be allowed to operate
unhindered. Aircraft were therefore equipped to attack
them; so war in the air began.

The bomber was in a slightly different category. Bombs
at this time were rudimentary, as were dropping
equipment and sights.

1915 therefore became a year of experimentation. As
specialist tasks appeared for the air services, so they had
to make do with adapting planes not really suitable for
their job. It was the Frenchman Roland Garros, a
well-known pre-war pilot, who first made effective use
of a Hotchkiss machine-gun firing through the propeller
of a Morane Saulnier L. There was no synchronization
but the propeller was protected by steel deflectors. Only
a short while later Garros was forced down in enemy
territory by engine failure. Anthony Fokker was shown
the device, with the result that Fokker's engineers
produced a synchronized gun which was fitted to the
Fokker E1, and the Allies suffered what was known as
the 'Fokker Scourge'.

The names that the Fokker monoplane also made
famous were those of Max Immelmann and Oswald
Boelcke, the first of the fighter 'aces'.

By 1918 military aircraft were divided into different
categories: the fighting scout, the reconnaissance machine,
the artillery observation plane, the day bomber and the
night bomber as well as the seaplane and the flying-boat.

In 1914 a Taube aircraft with a top speed of 70 mph and
a ceiling of 10,000 ft dropped five $6\frac{1}{2}$ lb bombs on Paris.
Four years later a DH 9A, with a ceiling of 17,000 ft, could
carry a bomb load of 460 lb at a top speed of 120 mph,
with a crew of two and three machine-guns.

It is surprising to record that the only American-built
aircraft to see combat in the First World War was a
British design, the DH 4. Yet the participation of
Americans in the air was perhaps their most important
contribution to the war. Stories of the feats of the
Escadrille Lafayette helped to bring the US into the
European conflict. Many Americans also served with the
RFC, but this service did not need to combine them in a
single unit, there being no language problem.

The use of the bomber involved the civilian population
in war as never before, especially in Britain; the Zeppelin
raids and later those of the Gothas had an impact far
beyond their material damage. Squadrons had to be
brought home from France, and much material and
manpower used to convince the public that they were
being adequately defended. It also brought into being a
philosophy of air power that was to influence the whole of
military and political thinking between the two world
wars. This estimate of the power of the bomber over the
civilian population was to alter the course of the Second
World War. It was because of this belief in air power that
1918 saw the formation of the independent Air Force, free
of actual Army control, pursuing a policy of strategic
bombing under the command of General Trenchard.

The golden years of flying

When the war ended the Allies deployed over four
thousand aircraft in Europe, and new squadrons were
being formed all the time. The number of aircraft on order
for the United States ran into tens of thousands.

The years between the wars are thought by many to be the
real summer of aviation for the lack of control by the

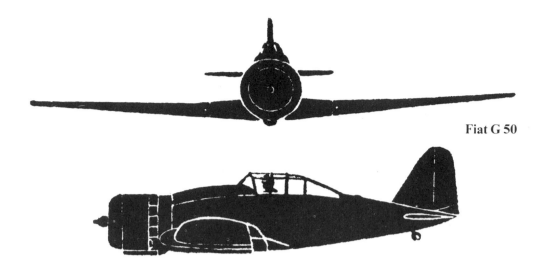

Fiat G 50

authorities allowed the pilot almost unlimited freedom to experiment.

The war was only over a short time before the trail blazers set out on their first high adventure. In May 1919 an American Curtiss NC 4 flew the Atlantic by stages, and in June Alcock and Brown made the first non-stop flight in a Vickers Vimy. A Vimy also won the Australian Government's £10,000 prize for a flight from England to Australia, piloted by Ross Smith and Keith Smith during November-December. Also in a Vimy, Pierre Van Ryneveld and Quintin Brand set out for Cape Town; but after crashing both this and another Vimy, they finally reached Cape Town in a DH 9 on the 20th March 1920.

France was at this time well in the lead in developing her airline services, though it was Germany which had started the first scheduled service between Berlin and Weimar. The first regular service is generally considered to be that by Air Transport and Travel Ltd, between London and Paris in August 1919, in a converted DH 4.

In the USA interest did not turn to passenger services, perhaps because the time gained was little over the very efficient transcontinental railroad, but an airmail service flying by both night and day did offer great advantages; the story of the US Mail Service is one of the great sagas in the history of flying. Day and night, sometimes in appalling weather, the mail pilots kept a regular schedule. Taking 34 hours 20 minutes westbound and 29 hours 15 minutes eastbound, planes and pilots were changed six times en route.

One of the great interests of the 1920s was a return to air race meetings. They took place in many countries and were a great incentive to designers at a time when governments were willing to make do with the aircraft they had.

Two important races which had been suspended during the war were the James Gordon Bennett Cup for land planes and the Schneider Trophy for seaplanes. The French won the Gordon Bennett Cup outright after their third successive win in 1920. Main interest now focused on the Schneider Trophy, as after the American official team won in 1923 it became an international affair between governments. The winning plane nearly always

went on to hold the world speed record. It was in 1927 that the first win for the Supermarine floatplanes, the S5/25 N220, was recorded. The S6 N247 Supermarine won again in 1929. The world financial crisis intervened before the next race, and the British Government decided that they could not find the money for a British entry despite the chance to win the trophy outright by a third win. Lady Houston came forward, however, with a cheque for £100,000 and the High Speed Flight was allowed to compete. The S6 B, designed by R. K. Mitchell, the designer of all the Supermarine winners, had a walk-over as the Italian entry was not ready. From the S6B and its Rolls-Royce engine came the Spitfire and the Merlin – perhaps the best spent £100,000 in history.

An important aspect of the air scene between the wars was the private pilot. In the 1920s, the ex-service pilot appeared, giving joy-rides in surplus ex-trainers purchased cheaply from the Government, using any suitable field around the country. In England the machine was frequently the Avro 504, while in the USA it was generally the ubiquitous 'Jenny' based on the design of Glen Curtiss. Often much altered by others, the 'Jenny' was used by the 'barnstormers' to thrill the public before authority caught up, and rules and regulations were brought in for the sake of safe flying.

Meanwhile, the early long distance flights made national heroes of Charles Lindberg, Dieudonné Costes, and General Balbo, and the British heroine, Amy Johnson.

The interest in private flying could not be denied, and the manufacturers realized the need for a special machine for the private pilot. By far the most successful of these was the DH Moth which appeared in 1925 at a price of £595. This machine and the other Moths that followed made the name of Moth synonymous with light planes.

The converted or developed bomber gave place to original bomber design. The leaders in this were Fokker with his high-wing monoplanes, and Junkers with his low-wing machines. Britain and France were more conservative in their approach, perhaps because the services were still the biggest customers of their aviation industries.

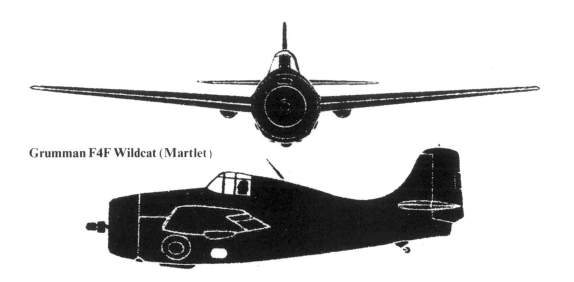

Grumman F4F Wildcat (Martlet)

One type of aircraft that was very important between the wars was the flying-boat. The philosophy that water offered the best aerodrome around the world was sound; Britain with her world commitments, and the USA with the vast expanses of the Pacific and Atlantic, both developed this type of aircraft. In fact the flying-boat dominated the long-range services during the years just before the Second World War, as epitomized by the Short Empire boats and the Sikorsky flying-boats of Pan-American which opened up the routes to South America. Flying-boats were used in the experimental transatlantic services shortly before the war.

There were signs, however, that the landplane was about to challenge the seaplane, and already one of the world's great planes was entering service – the Douglas DC 3. Douglas's challenge to the European manufacturers highlighted the American entry into the passenger-carrying side of civil aviation. By now the airplane had developed sufficiently to take the place of the train as the best method of long-distance travel in the United States.

The different approach to airplane design between the military and civil requirements is shown by the fact that the Boeing 247 with a retractable undercarriage in 1933 was in service while the first RAF bomber with such an undercarriage entered service in 1937. But the British were by no means unusual in being so conservative. The Fiat Cr 42 Falco, a biplane single-seat fighter with a fixed undercarriage, was ordered into production in 1939.

To give an idea of the progress over two decades, the speed record for 1929 was 357.73 mph (Britain); height 41,749 ft (Germany); and distance in a straight line 4,912 miles (France). In 1939 they were respectively 469.142 mph (Germany); 56,046 ft (Italy); and 7,158 miles (Britain).

The fighter remained based on the small manoeuvrable biplane: in France there was the highly successful Nieuport-Delage 29 which held several records and also saw service in Italy and Japan; in Britain the Sopwith Snipe remained the front line fighter for several years, until replaced by the Armstrong-Whitworth Siskin and Gloster Grebe. The US Army decided on the design of

the Thomas Morse MB 3 with a 340 hp Wright-Hispano engine, and as the accepted design was then the property of the Army they awarded the contract for the production of two hundred – the largest production order for fighters until 1937 – to Boeing, and the machine became known as the Boeing MB 3a. The MB 3a was followed by the Curtiss Hawks, one of the most famous designs between the wars. Boeing remained a strong competitor for contracts and they produced a landmark in the P 26, the Army's first monoplane fighter, although it still had a fixed undercarriage.

The naval air arms of Britain and the United States, in the 1920s the only major powers operating aircraft-carriers, required specialized machines for this purpose. Two famous types during this period were the Fairey Flycatcher in Britain and the Boeing F4B series in the United States. The first mark of the Boeing entered service in 1929, and some of the later marks were still on charge at training establishments in 1941. During the same period a series of high-wing monoplane fighters were produced in France, such as the Wibaults and the Dewoitines, while in Italy the very successful series of Fiat fighters first entered service. France at this time was producing some interesting bomber prototypes, though for economic reasons only one or two entered service.

Britain was producing both day and night bombers, the most famous of the former being the Hawker Hart, which was faster than contemporary fighters. Little attention was given to the development of the night bomber, and the Vickers Virginia, serving from 1924–37, with a maximum speed of 108 mph, was only a few miles an hour faster than the Vimy of 1918. The troop-carrying version, the Victoria, operated the first major airlift when some hundreds of civilians and their baggage were evacuated from Kabul at Christmas 1928, during local riots.

Though Trenchard as Chief of Air Staff of the RAF believed in the heavy bomber, in America its advocate, Brigadier-General 'Billy' Mitchell, ran into such trouble with his superiors that he was forced to resign from the Army Air Corps. It was, however, the United States which produced in the Martin B 10, the forerunner of the monoplane bombers of the Second World War.

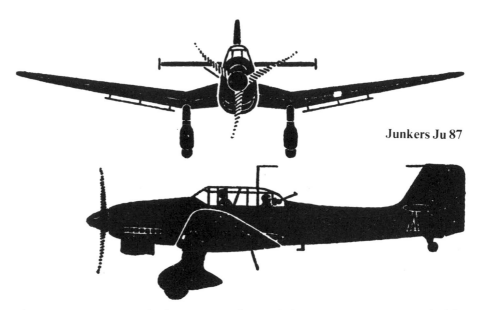

Junkers Ju 87

In the short history of aviation there has always seemed to be slow periods of development followed by a sudden revolutionary movement in design. Such was the pattern in the late 1930s, with the appearance of low wing monoplanes, retractable undercarriages and enclosed cockpits, and the disappearance of the biplane from the aviation scene. Aviation is ruthless to its failures, and so the biplane went the way of the airship; but it had served its pilots well, and many people felt that real flying died with the biplane.

Second World War: the great air battles

During the Spanish Civil War the German Air Force, the Luftwaffe, had worked out a new pattern of support for an army. This new pattern, used by the Condor Legion supporting General Franco, was fitted in to the German Army's idea of the Blitzkrieg itself, which was based partly on the teachings of British tank experts and partly on the method of attack that had nearly won in 1918.

When Germany attacked Poland on 1st September, 1939, the new ideas had their first real test. The Heinkel He 111 and Dornier Do 17 twin-engined bombers attacked enemy airfields and vital points like bridges and railroad junctions, causing the maximum confusion in the enemy's rear. These bombers were escorted by fighters who, once their charges had turned safely for home, would dive down to strafe anything that moved. While these attacks were going on, the Ju 87 squadrons were giving close support to the advancing troops attacking strong points and Polish troops. The Polish Air Force, outclassed and outnumbered, could do little to help its Army and soon ceased to offer any resistance. The theories in Spain were considered proved – and so was the might of the new Luftwaffe.

Later, in Norway, the Luftwaffe again had the skies to itself, except for a few planes operating from a frozen lake. Holland, Belgium and France fell and Göring believed that there was nothing that his air force could not achieve. Perhaps Dunkirk should have made him think

again, because surely no air force was ever presented with a better target than those exposed troops on the beaches. Göring had no doubt of the outcome when the Battle of Britain commenced – nor did most of the waiting world.

The RAF, however, was now fighting on its own ground, doing the job it had been designed to do, with aircraft that were just as good as its opponents: better armed, and supported by the only fighter direction system then in use. The outcome was 'a near run thing'; all the books since written agree that it could have gone either way. If the German fighters had been given more freedom from close escort, if the range of the 109 had been greater . . . but all the battles of history have been won and lost on ifs. All we can say now is that the Luftwaffe was beaten in the purest air battle in history.

Out of that battle a legend was born and the name 'Spitfire' became synonymous with the hope of freedom. It served from the beginning of the war to the end, on all fronts and in all climates, even taking to the sea on aircraft carriers and becoming the Seafire. From those seaplanes racing around the Schneider pylons there had come an even more beautiful machine. Perhaps the secret of the Spitfire's appeal is that it was one of the most beautiful airplanes ever built, and the sky seemed so naturally its element.

1939–45 was a forcing house for the aircraft designer. Often hindered by bureaucracy and private feuds, each strove to give his country the weapon to win the battle, but the nation with the best aircraft does not necessarily win the battle. Electronics are now such a major factor that the work of the back-room scientist, who may not even see his invention, can change a whole battle.

The story of the most successful American fighter of the war, the North American P 51 Mustang, is perhaps the best example of many inventive threads coming together to make the perfect weave. Designed at the request of the British Purchasing Commission before Japan's attack on Pearl Harbor, it was evaluated by the USAAF and ordered as an attack fighter. The Allison engine with which it was fitted did not give sufficient power at height, and the aircraft was used first by the RAF as a low level army co-operation and photo-reconnaissance machine.

Boeing B 17 Flying Fortress

But it was so popular with its pilots, and so much the best American single-seater to reach the RAF, that efforts were made to improve its performance. Four aircraft were given Rolls Royce Merlin engines, and the result was so successful that plans were immediately put in hand for P 51s in the States to be fitted with the Packard-built Merlin. The success of the P 51B is well known, but before it was complete another change was to take place: the adoption of the computer gun-sight, a tremendous aid to marksmanship in the air.

In 1940, shortly after Italy had declared war, Fleet Air Arm Swordfish torpedo bombers attacked and crippled three Italian battleships in harbour at Taranto, neutralizing the Italian fleet for several months. This was the first time a battle fleet was knocked out by a single air raid. It was not to be the last.

In 1941 German airborne forces carried out an invasion of Crete and occupied the island, defended by New Zealand and British troops who were supported only by the Royal Navy. German air command forced the British to give up the island.

The end of the year was to see the airplane being used to full effect with the Japanese attack on Pearl Harbor and the destruction of HMS *Prince of Wales* and HMS *Repulse*. If the Americans had lost their carriers as well as their battleships, the outcome of the war might have been very different. The effectiveness of the Japanese attacks was increased by the aircraft they used. The Mitsubishi A 6M Zero-Sen (code name 'Zeke') was a considerable shock to the Allies as, in the hands of the experienced Japanese Navy pilots, it was a match for any Allied aircraft.

In the summer of 1942 there occurred the battles of the Coral Sea and Midway – the first sea battles in which the two fleets never saw each other, the fighting being done by aircraft. In the Coral Sea fight the Americans lost the carrier *Lexington* but learned many valuable lessons; and a broken Japanese code enabled them to position *Yorktown*, *Enterprise* and *Hornet* to intercept the Japanese fleet heading for Midway Atoll. In two days of air fighting the Americans lost the *Yorktown* – but without radar the Japanese were wide open to surprise enemy attacks. Four Japanese carriers were sunk, and

with the Japanese defeat at Midway the tide of the Pacific War turned.

In Europe, Britain had embarked on a policy of strategic bombing, partly because it was the only way she could hit back at Germany, and partly because she had already in production the three types of four-engined bombers that had been designed to carry out such attacks by night. The most successful of these was the Lancaster, ably supported by the later marks of Halifax; the Stirling was eventually used for other duties with the airborne forces and Transport Command.

The Americans also had faith in strategic bombing, but by day, believing that their heavily armed Fortress and Liberator bombers could fight their way to the target. This was not possible, but eventually they were able to make the major contribution with their bombers escorted by Thunderbolts, Lightnings and, most effective of all, Mustangs.

The Allies also built up a Tactical Air Force to support ground troops, based on the experience gained by the Desert Air Force in Africa. This force used medium bombers, like the Mitchell and Marauder, and rocket-firing fighters, such as the Typhoon, which made it impossible for the German Army to move by day in Normandy. When necessary Allied heavy bombers were used in support of particular actions, with spectacular results.

A further force was needed in the Battle of the Atlantic. RAF Coastal Command had specialized needs and produced its own special aircraft. In the early days it used flying-boats like the Short Sunderland, based on the design of Imperial Airways Empire flying-boats; later it discovered that long-range land-based aircraft could serve as well. Armstrong Whitworth Whitleys were converted, followed by Wellingtons, Fortresses and, perhaps most successfully, Liberators. These aircraft first escorted convoys, and then on offensive patrols made the U-boat's journey to and from its hunting grounds as dangerous as an attack on a convoy.

The U-boat was not the only danger the convoys had to face. There were attacks from the Luftwaffe, using Focke-Wulf Condor or the Heinkel He 177 which was

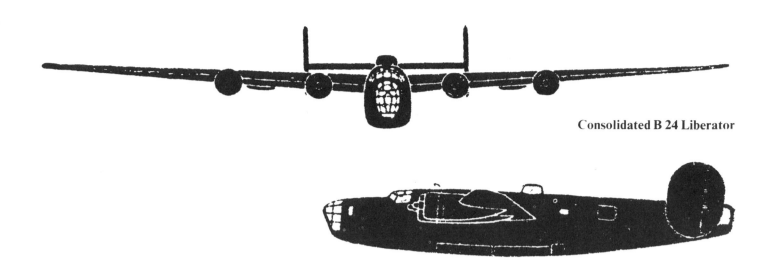

Consolidated B 24 Liberator

Germany's only attempt to produce a long-range bomber. Two successful night fighters, the Bristol Beaufighter and the De Havilland Mosquito, were used as long-range fighters. Convoys with their own escorts of Grummond Wildcats or Hurricanes flying from escort carriers sometimes used torpedoes or six-pounder guns against German shipping.

Perhaps the most advanced and sophisticated production aircraft to come from the United States during the Second World War was the Boeing B 29 Superfortress, with its pressurized circular section fuselage, remote-controlled turrets, and an ability to carry 10,000 lb of bombs at 30,000 ft to a target 1,500 miles away. The effect of war on aircraft development is well illustrated by the comparison between the attack by hundreds of B 29s on the Japanese mainland and that single Taube over Paris thirty years earlier in August 1914.

Air transport had become a vital part of the war effort. In 1939 the flying of the Atlantic by one mail plane was headline news; by the end of the war hundreds of aircraft had been delivered to Britain across 'the pond', and whole squadrons of the USAAF had used this route to reach the European Theatre of Operations.

It was this transport revolution, based on the Dakota (C 47), Skymaster (C 54), and Curtiss Commando (C 46), that was to have a tremendous impact after the war. Routes had been pioneered around the globe, and the Pacific crossing had become commonplace.

The air power of the British and Americans may have been decisive in the Second World War, though their ally Russia suffered through lack of command in the air till near the end of her 'Great Patriotic War'. Many of the most revolutionary ideas and machines, however, were devised in Germany. Not only were the Germans the first to build up a jet fighter force, but they had in the Arado 234 and Junkers 287, the first jet bombers, and in the Messerschmitt Me 163 the first rocket fighter, as well as ingenious designs like the 'people's fighter', the Heinkel He 162.

The speed of piston engined fighters had gone up by fifty per cent and their engine power had doubled. Bomb loads had gone up as much as five times, and the bombers'

range had more than doubled. The .303-inch machine gun was disappearing and the 20-mm cannon was taking its place in the Allied air forces; the Germans were already producing 30-mm cannon. Everything was larger and heavier and stronger and over them all hung the shadow of the mushroom cloud.

Into the jet age

After the Japanese surrender in 1945, peace offered great opportunities to airline companies for a world-wide network of air transportation. The machines that were used in the first few post-war years were a very motley collection. American planes dominated the scene, the United States being the only country that had been producing transport aircraft. Britain brought into service several stopgaps using bomber conversions, like the Lancastrian, which were expensive to operate and basically unsatisfactory. France also made use of sequestered German wartime transports, including that great work-horse of the Luftwaffe, the Ju 52. Russia had been producing the Li 2, its version of the DC 3, and in 1947 brought into service its first post-war aircraft, the Ilyushin Il 12. This was superseded in 1954 by the Il 14 (a modified Il 12).

In America there were many surplus DC 4s in service and these were soon augmented by the larger and more powerful version, the pressurized DC 6. Many DC 4s, 6s, and the later DC 7, are still being used by charter and freight firms. The DCs helped America dominate the long range transport market during the 1950s, aided by two other planes, the Boeing Stratocruiser – perhaps the most comfortable passenger aircraft of its time – and the graceful Constellation.

The Brabazon Committee had recommended a series of designs to the United Kingdom government; one to be an expensive failure like its namesake the Bristol Brabazon, and one to be a best seller. This was the turbo-prop Vickers Viscount, whose smooth and quiet engines brought a new kind of comfort to medium distance travel. The success of this machine, sold to operators all over the world, caused interest to be focused on the

Handley Page Halifax

turbo-prop airliner. It was followed by the Vickers Vanguard and Bristol Britannia in the United Kingdom, the Lockheed Electra in the USA, and the Ilyushin Il 16 in Russia. Japan's successful entry into the post-war market, the NAMC YS 11, has a pair of Rolls Royce Dart engines, like the Viscount.

The United Kingdom was justly proud when the De Havilland Comet, the world's first jet airliner, entered service in 1952. These unfortunately had to be grounded following tragic accidents, but the improved Comets were the first to start a North Atlantic jet service. The Boeing 707 was hard on the heels, though in fact a Russian machine, the Tupolev Tu 104, was the second passenger jet in use.

The success of the 707/720 was overwhelming, and Boeing has since supplied hundreds to all the world's long-distance passenger carriers. Perhaps the only people to benefit from this change-over were charter operators, who were able to buy many piston-engined airliners at a knock-down price. Douglas came into the market later with its DC 8, and Convair with the 880. Only the Russians with their giant Tupolev Tu 114 remained faithful to the turbo-prop, and the 14,795 hp Kuznetsov was the most powerful engine in the world.

During the 1950s France had been working hard to reclaim her place in civil aviation, but it was not until the Caravelle appeared that she achieved her deserved success. The first of the rear-engined airliners, the Caravelle, had two Rolls Royce Avons, and the clean wing which has become the norm in airliner design.

Russia and the United Kingdom are the only two countries to produce aircraft with four engines at the tail. Boeing, when it produced its 'jumbo' 747, put the engines under the wings as on the 707. When this great machine was announced there were many Cassandras foretelling the troubles, and tragedies, of so many hundreds of people in one machine. It is true that the seating has generally been cut to around 370 rather than the original figure of nearly 500, but the handling organization problems have been overcome and there are now over two hundred completed or on order. There are three more air buses on the scene, the unlucky

TriStar and the McDonnell Douglas DC 10, each with three rear-mounted engines, and the European venture the A 300B with two wing pods – perhaps too much competition for the market.

Supersonic transport remains the big question mark. BOAC have announced orders for the BAC-Aerospatiale Concorde, and Aeroflot, the Russian airline, says it hopes to have the Tu 144 in service by 1974. Other airlines are at the moment (1972) hanging back, partly perhaps because of the doubtful economics but also because of the environmentalists' attack. Since a number of orders have been announced, however, it seems that the odds may be shifting in Concorde's favour.

A new class of aircraft that has appeared on the commercial scene since the war is the business or executive plane for the use of companies or even rich individuals. Special small jets like the Hawker Siddeley 125 or Dessault Mystère 10, again with rear-mounted engines, have been produced to satisfy this market. Private flying in Europe has failed to regain its pre-war place possibly because the speed and number of scheduled flights over Europe make strict control of movement very necessary. In Russia and the Americas it is still very popular, though reports of mid-air collisions in the United States make it likely that even there the freedom of the private pilot may soon be limited.

New advances in military aircraft

The end of the Second World War did not mean a complete halt in the production of new military aircraft. This was partly because the Western Allies wished to develop machines with the British jet engines, and to exploit German discoveries which had come into their hands. Also America was determined, after Pearl Harbor, never to be caught unprepared again. After Korea, factories were soon back in production with both tried and new aircraft. One of the first discoveries of the Korean War was that the limited endurance of the new jets presented many problems when support was needed

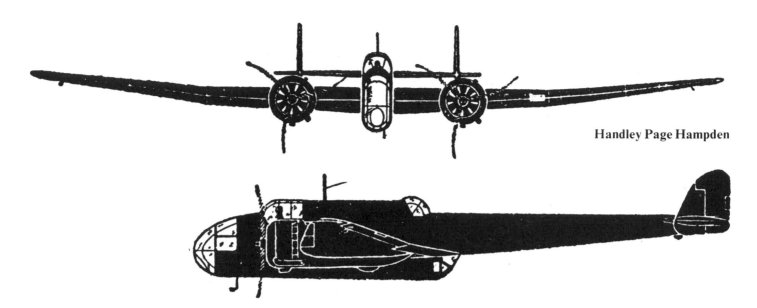

Handley Page Hampden

by ground troops; piston-driven aircraft were able to remain airborne for longer. In Normandy the RAF had worked out a highly efficient 'cab-rank' system which meant that support was always on call. It was solved by bringing back, for tactical support, well-tried Second World War machines like the Corsair, Mustang, Attacker and Invader.

Nearer the Chinese border a new kind of air war was being fought, the first to use jets on both sides. At first, to the discomfort of the Americans, the Russian-built MiG 15s were superior, but western air supremacy was regained with the appearance of the North American F 86 Sabre. The Sabre was the fighter of the 1950s, and it served with nearly all the NATO Air Forces including the RAF, RCAF and Italian Air Force. In 1965 later marks of Sabre were still serving with the US Air National Guard, and they serve with the Air Forces of many smaller nations today. When it first entered service the Sabre was armed with six .5-inch machine guns like Second World War fighters, but the last marks had four 20-mm cannon and two Sidewinder missiles. In all, more than eight thousand Sabres have been built.

Sheer cost has become the main feature in developing a new aircraft. The expense is so great that European nations have found it impossible to do on their own, and consortiums have been set up between nations and international companies to produce new machines. Among these joint ventures is the Franco-British Jaguar, the British-German-Italian MRCA, and a new training aircraft which is being worked on by the French and Germans. It is this cost that has made possible the Russo-American agreement to limit the arms race.

One of the important developments during the 1960s was work on swing-wing aircraft based on the work of Sir Barnes Wallis of 'Dambuster bomb' fame, the principle being that this type of wing can have the best aerodynamic position for landing and high-speed flight. The Americans chose it for the General Dynamics F 111, which was to have been supplied to both the Air Force and the Navy. The Russians have shown two at fly-pasts; one by Mikoyan (code name 'Flogger') is believed to have entered service; and the French have produced one in the Mirage G. New products like the MRCA and the Grumman F 14 Tomcat have swing wings, but the biggest of all will be the North American Rockwall B 1. This new American strategic bomber is about as large as a 707, and the prototype is due to fly some time in 1974.

The long-range bomber force armed with nuclear weapons – Strategic Air Command (SAC) – was formed in 1946. It was first equipped with B 29s and later the B 50; and for many years it used the Convair B 36, the second largest aircraft that has ever served in the USAF, with a wing span of 230 ft and a length of 162 ft. The later versions had ten engines, six 3,500 hp Pratt and Witney piston engines driving pusher propellers, and four jet engines, two slung under the end of each wing. When it was retired from SAC in 1959 the Force became solely jet-equipped. One B 36/H was modified to carry a nuclear reactor to investigate shielding problems in aircraft and the effect of radiation on instrumentation.

The first jet to enter service with SAC was the B 47 Stratojet in 1951. This can be said to be the first fully operational jet bomber. It had laminar-flow wings swept back at an angle of 35 degrees, with three engines under each wing, and with a crew of three it could carry a 20,000 lb internal bomb load at a maximum speed of just over 600 mph. Since 1966 it has been replaced by the B 56 and the mighty B 52. The present equipment of SAC consists of the B 52 and the General Dynamics FB 111.

Britain's most successful bomber since the war has been the English Electric Canberra. This medium bomber has just been phased out of the RAF but continues to serve in eight other Air Forces, together with the Martin B 57, a United States built version which is still used for jamming enemy radar.

Before it was handed over to the Royal Navy, the delivery of British nuclear weapons was the job of the V-Bomber Force, with their four jet Valiants, Victors and Vulcan. The Vickers Valiant is no longer in service; the Handley Page Victor is now used as a flight refuelling tanker (a method of air refuelling which was developed by Britain to solve the short endurance of jet aircraft); and the Avro Vulcan is now primarily used in a support role.

With the products of Marcel Dassault, France has

Heinkel He 111

returned to her place as one of the most successful countries which produce military aircraft. The Dassault Mirage III 5, Milan and the new F 1 are basically fighter aircraft, while the Mirage IV A is a larger bomber version for France's nuclear weapons. The earlier Mystère still serves with the Israeli Air Force.

There have been a series of small wars since Korea in which aircraft have taken part. Among these have been two Indo-Pakistan conflicts and two Israeli-Arab wars. In the latter, tactical air surprise was so complete that the Arab Air Forces were unable to get off the ground. In the Indian subcontinent perhaps the greatest success was achieved by the little Folland Gnat of the Indian Force, a lightweight fighter that is highly manoeuvrable. Light attack aircraft are becoming very popular as they are much cheaper than their highly sophisticated, heavier counterparts, and as they can also serve in their original training role. Examples are the Aermacchi MB 326, the Cessna A 37, BAC Jet Provost and the Saab 105. They are mainly used in a COIN (counter insurgency) role which presupposes command of the air.

As has been stated, the developments of the USSR have come as a shock to the West. Their large turbo-prop aircraft like the Tupolev Tu 95 and transports like the Antonov An 22 are most impressive. The MiG 23 (Foxbat) which has appeared over Egypt appears to be faster than any contemporary Western machine in service, with a Mach 3 capability.

Now that the fan-jet or turbo-prop has given the designer such apparently unlimited amounts of power, at least ten times as much per engine as was available in 1945, military transports have been produced of truly mammoth size. The Lockheed Galaxy has flown at a gross weight of 798,200 lb (over 350 tons) at a top speed of 570 mph. The Russian An 22 is a good deal smaller but can still carry a payload of over eight tons at 450 mph. The Russian ability to deploy a large number of troops and vehicles by air during the Czechoslovakian crisis of 1968 has given Western military planners a new headache; this mobility is an important factor in military planning.

It is now possible to see how far the aeroplane has come in less than seventy years since that day at Kitty

Hawk. It is one of the major methods of world transportation, and every year thousands of people travel millions of miles around the globe. Although associated in some people's minds with war's worst horrors, it has been responsible for saving thousands of lives. It is never correct to blame an instrument for man's injustices to man; however it is certain that the airplane – correctly used – will bring people closer together and help to make the only world we have a peaceful one.

Aircraft in miniature

Models have played an important part in the development of the airplane from the earliest times, helping the inventor to give his ideas a practical form without risking his life. An important invention came in 1872 when Francis Wenham and John Browning produced the wind tunnel, in which a model can be placed and its behaviour studied. The Wright brothers built a small wind tunnel in which they tried out hundreds of ideas for their 'Flyer'.

During the First World War models were used to train pilots and observers in aerial gunnery, sometimes in a machine rather like a funfair shooting gallery, sometimes carried around at the end of a long pole. The trainee gunner's task was to keep the moving model in his gun-sights.

After 1918 the two hobbies of flying modelling and display modelling grew together. The models selected to illustrate the history of the airplane in this book all belong to the non-flying, display category.

The first scale models were made in wood. This material demands considerable time and skill to be fashioned into a satisfactory model, and has usually been reserved for the most confirmed enthusiast. Next appeared cardboard cut-outs, which could produce quite satisfactory models – and then, in the early 1930s, came the famous Skybird kits.

In a Skybird kit the fuselage and wings were rough-hewn in wood for the modeller to finish with other metal parts (such as engine, exhaust and guns). A Skybird League, with some hundreds of club branches, was formed. These branches were mainly British, though there

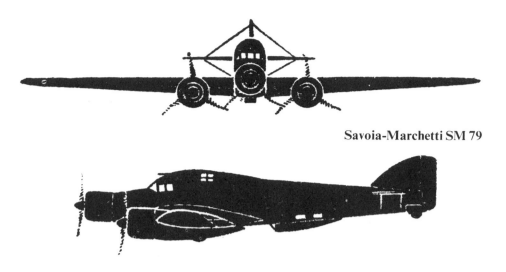

Savoia-Marchetti SM 79

were some abroad. Local competitions were held, with a national competition in London every year. The Skybird range was expanded to include pilots, mechanics, hangars, control towers and the like. Model dioramas were much more popular than today – perhaps because the wooden models were stronger and could stand up to more handling. Reference information, so essential to a modeller, was provided by *Skybird Magazine*, later merged with *Aero-Modellist*. In addition there was *Air Stories*, which as well as publishing fictional and factual articles each month included features by James Hay Stevens, the original designer of Skybird kits, with scale plans of famous aircraft and tips for the modeller.

Late in the 1930s came the Frog Penguin plastic kits, very detailed, made from acetate – but these disappeared with the outbreak of the Second World War. Skybirds were still produced in small numbers but they were difficult to obtain, and the firm went bankrupt shortly after the end of the war.

Wartime, and the obsession with accurate aircraft recognition, gave much stimulus to the making of high-quality models. Highly-skilled enthusiasts, both military and civilian, produced scratch-built models, many of which were to be seen in fund-raising displays.

After 1945 Penguins reappeared on the market at about the time of the disappearance of Skybirds, but they did not achieve much popularity – possibly because the moulding of the parts was not as good as in pre-war years. Several balsa-wood kits came on the market, but just as after the end of the First World War, it seemed that a few years had to pass before the modeller came into his own.

In 1952 the American firm of Lindberg started to produce polystyrene plastic kits, and Lindberg were soon followed by other American manufacturers. Something new, however, was achieved when Airfix began to produce their constant scale kits in 1954. The American kits had been produced in several scales – 1:72, 1:50, 1:46, and so on. Airfix, however, produced their high-quality plastic kits to the old scale of 1:72.

In 1963 a group of British modellers got together and formed the British Plastic Modellers Society. From

meetings at the 'Porcupine', a London public house, the society grew until by 1964 interest from overseas was so great that the name was changed to the International Plastic Modellers Society. The first overseas branch – which remains one of the most flourishing today – was in the United States. Subsequent branches were formed in Australia and Canada; and the European branches include Italy, West Germany, Austria, Norway, Sweden, and Finland. Branches have also been founded behind the Iron Curtain, in Poland and Czechoslovakia. In all there are active branches in some twenty countries, from Japan to Brazil.

The great advantage of plastic modelling is that the novice can start with a shop-bought kit, a tube of cement, three or four tins of paint and a couple of brushes, and so keep the cost of his early errors to the minimum. When he gains experience he can, if he wishes, increase his outlay with more expensive tools and accessories. Research information is vital to a keen modeller – especially if he later turns from kits to plastic card and the model really is his own creation – and most modellers build up their own libraries; but even the beginner can find much useful information on the shelves of his local public library.

Like the Skybird League, the IPMS holds competitions and has its own magazine; but the society is run by members for members, and has no obligations to any manufacturer. The magazine, which is sent monthly to every member, is of a very high standard and the reviews of new kits are excellent. There are always articles and pictures by members, full of helpful information. Several overseas branches also publish magazines, to which members may subscribe if they wish.

Manufactured kits today range in scale from 1:144 (the most popular scale for airliners) to 1:24 for single-seat fighters. But size is not necessarily a guide to accuracy: this can vary a great deal from kit to kit in the same range. Modelling standards today have reached a very high level, both with kit-based models and scratch-built ones; and the use of plastic card is becoming more and more popular. Inspired by the work of the finest modellers, the scope for the enthusiast is unlimited.

15

1

1–2 Wright 'Flyer' by Michael Moore (1:48 scale). The world's first successful heavier-than-air powered flying machine, it was catapulted into the air from a small trolley running on a railway. The pilot lay face down on the wing; later variations of the Flyer – such as the one taken to France by Wilbur Wright in 1908 – were fitted with a skeletal seat for the pilot, and another for the privileged passenger. The Flyer had a 40-foot wing span and was about 21 feet long; its 12 horse-power engine gave it a speed of around 30 mph depending on the strength of headwinds. Orville Wright made the first flight, on 17th December, 1903 – a distance of 120 feet in 12 seconds. On the last of three further flights that day, Wilbur was airborne for 51 seconds.

2

3 Voisin Box-Kite by Harry Woodman (1:48 scale). The Voisin was the first commercial aircraft produced in France. It was not a very original machine – the first powered Voisins lacked the lateral controls of the Wright Flyer – but it gained considerable popularity, and seven Voisins competed in the Reims meeting in August 1909. This model shows the 'Bird of Passage' which was ordered by Henri Farman but sold by the Voisin brothers to J. T. C. Moore-Brabazon, who gained Britain's pilot licence No 1. Henri Farman subsequently set up his own aircraft-building company. The Voisin had a 60 horse-power engine and a maximum speed of 34 mph.

4 Martin-Handasyde 3, by Harry Woodman (1:48 scale). This very attractive monoplane drew much attention when it appeared in 1910, and a larger machine was ordered by Britain's T. O. M. Sopwith. Just before the outbreak of war in 1914 the firm was working on a machine for Gustav Hamel's projected attempt to fly the Atlantic. The No 3 was fitted with several engines during its career, and had a maximum speed of 60 mph.

5 BE 2 by Bill Hearne (1:28 scale). A bridge between the experimental era in aviation and the first warplanes of the First World War, the BE 2 was an aircraft that was forced to do tasks for which it was never intended. It gained a bad reputation after the outbreak of hostilities as many BE 2 pilots were shot down, but this was not due to any fault in the plane's original design. A product of the British Royal Aircraft Factory during its search for an inherently stable aircraft – a machine which can be flown 'hands off' – the first BE 2 took to the air in 1912. The first aircraft of the Royal Flying Corps to land in France after the outbreak of war in 1914 was a BE 2A. Early experience gained in France showed that the original arrangement of a pilot in the rear cockpit and an observer in the front was unsatisfactory, and this was changed on the BE 2D; but for some reason the BE 2E reverted to the former design – an example of the bad liaison between pilots and aircraft designers. However the BE 2 scored several successes in Home Defence duties in England, and was credited with the destruction of four Zeppelins and a Schutte-Lanz airship. The BE 2E, illustrated here, had a maximum speed of 82 mph.

6 Bristol 'Box-Kite' by R. Rowley (1:48 scale). An obvious copy of the contemporary Farman III by Bristol, this was a very successful design in the years 1910–13. Just as Henri Farman had improved on the Voisin, so G. H. Challenger, the Bristol designer, improved on the Farman. It was a popular trainer.

7 Morane-Saulnier N by Harry Woodman (1:48 scale). With its clean appearance and streamlined outline, the Morane-Saulnier N was years ahead of its time, but this did not apply to its armament. Like its predecessor, the L, it had an unsynchronized forward-firing machine-gun, whose bullets were deflected from the propeller blades by metal plates.

8 Fokker Monoplane by Harry Woodman (1:48 scale). The 'Fokker Scourge' was the first aircraft to be fitted with an interrupter gear to prevent its bullets from hitting the propeller. The Fokker E III was by far the most numerous of the three marks produced, and was supplied to Austria and Turkey. Some versions had two or even three Spandau machine-guns. It was on these aircraft that Boelcke and Immelmann, the first two German aces, made their names between the summer of 1915 and the spring of 1916.

9 FE 8 by Tony Woollett (1:72 scale). This was the pattern of aircraft design which put an end to the 'Fokker Scourge'. Like the DH 2, the FE 8 was a 'pusher' machine, resulting from the lack of a synchronized machine-gun which could fire forwards through the propeller.

8

9

10

11

12

10–15 Selected models by the American modeller Paul E. Parker of New York, who specializes in the camouflage schemes of First World War planes.

10 An excellent reproduction of the Pfalz D XII, serial number D 2600/18, which can still be viewed at the Australian War Memorial, Canberra. Though it illustrates the typical camouflage pattern common to many German fighters of its time, its two camouflage schemes – one on the fuselage, one on the flying surfaces – have provided accurate data for students of First World War colourings. The first, on the fuselage, is the irregular scheme of several colours, applied with a spray gun. Photographs show that many German planes used this technique, but the only known example to have survived which offers sufficiently conclusive colour information is the one on this Pfalz fighter. The second, the five-colour lozenge pattern, is important to researchers because it provided material for the first definitive study of this type of camouflage. This information was first published in 1958, and is in wide use by plane restorers and modellers alike. The scheme had two colour arrangements: darker colours for the top and side surfaces and lighter colours for the undersurfaces. Almost certainly, this Pfalz was covered with the latter scheme only.

11 The Fokker Dr I triplane was made famous by many German pilots, the most celebrated of which was Manfred von Richthofen – the 'Red Baron'. There is no certainty that he actually flew an all-red plane since no photographic evidence exists of it, despite the fact that his last triplane – 425/17 – was described by him as a 'red aircraft'. Students of First World War colourings, however, have learned that such a brief description does not often mean what it implies. But the triplane shown by this model, Richthofen's 152/17, is well documented by photographs and specific areas coloured red are mentioned in one of his battle reports. The top wing has been completely covered with a dark red; the engine cowling, wheel covers, inter-plane struts, the rear fuselage section and the tail assembly have been painted in the same colour. The remainder is representative of factory-finish colouring: streaky green and grey camouflage with medium-blue under-surfaces. Richthofen flew at least seven different triplanes but one of the most famous was Fl 102/17, the second production plane, delivered to Richthofen by Fokker himself during acceptance trials in August 1917. At this time the machine carried no red colours at all, but it is possible that when Richthofen began flying it in battle in September 1917 or thereabouts it carried red on its engine cowling and tail.

12 This model shows a Fokker D VII of *Jasta* 15. The fighter was brought down by British SE 5s of No 24 Squadron near Couchy on June 17, 1918. The German pilot, *Leutnant* Wustoff, was not the owner; he had borrowed the plane from *Leutnant* Hantelmann, whose personal insignia was the death's head. *Jasta* 15 belonged to *Jagdgeschwader* 2 which was commanded by *Oberleutnant* Rudolph Berthold, who had ordered all units under his command to be identified by the colour of his former infantry regiment. Henceforth all planes of his units had their fuselages and tail assemblies painted blue, with the individual *Jastas* using different colours on the nose and the front part of the fuselage. *Jasta* 15 was assigned red. Here the wings are covered with four-colour lozenge fabric, over-painted with the 'Greek cross' national emblem. Notice how the fuselage cross has been painted over with blue and not restored – a condition typical of this *Geschwader*. The serial number – 1445/18 – has suffered a similar fate, but in this case it is no longer visible. It was determined after the plane was shot down and inspected by the British.

13 This Fokker D VIII (serial number 132/18) of an unknown *Jasta* is a good example of the colour scheme of a factory-delivered plane. Apart from the white stripes on the tailplane, a black surround on the fin and rudder, and the white band behind the cockpit, its appearance is the same as when it was passed for delivery by the Fokker *Flugzeugwerke* Gmbh. It is entirely covered with the standard four-colour lozenge fabric – except, of course, for the wing struts and engine cowling, which are painted grey. For a more gaily-decorated scheme for this plane, modellers should remember *Jasta* 6 of the 'Richthofen' *Geschwader* 1. Even after Richthofen's death, the unit carried black and white as its distinguishing colours. The *Jasta* 6 D VIIIs had black and white 'petal' designs on their engine cowlings along with black and white striped tailplanes and wheel covers. Individual pilot markings were located on the fuselage near the Greek cross and featured such devices as an arrow or a bolt of lightning.

14 The Roland D VIb was noted, among its other features, for its *klinkerrumpf* fuselage construction, a style similar to that of small boats. With its keel-mounted lower wing and low-slung nose, the Roland D VIb presented a rather distinguished appearance, although there was nothing remarkable about its flying qualities. The plane shown by this model – serial number 6117/18 – is a production machine. There is, for example, no device depicting a specific *Jasta* or individual pilot on its natural wood finish – a condition which was quite usual. The really gaudy German planes were often the exception, not the rule. The wing surfaces carry the five-colour lozenge pattern, as do the wheel covers. The engine cowling and the 'saxophone' exhaust pipe are coloured grey, and the wing struts have been left in a natural wood colour. The national insignia is the Greek cross (*Balkankreuz*), which was ordered to replace the *Patée* cross in April 1918.

15 This Löhner-built Knoller C II two-seater (serial number 115.15) is a good example of Austro-Hungarian camouflage design and colouration. The model is the result of carefully detailed colour studies made in the Prague Technological Museum, where the original plane still exists in good condition. This colour design was painted on the plane, as opposed to the German practice of the time which used printed colour fabric. Note the interesting demarcation of the colours on the fuselage and wings. The boundaries they form were subsequently used when the Austrians decided to use only two colours – dark green and khaki – for concealment purposes. The Berg fighter in the Technical Museum near Vienna is a fine example of this development. The undersurfaces of this plane were a light but vivid blue with khaki wings and stabilizer. The struts were painted in medium grey, but the radiator was left in its original brass colour. The *Patée* crosses are without the usual white outline.

16 SE5 A Scout by Norman Whitcomb (1:72 scale). The SE5 A ties with the Sopwith Camel as the best British fighter of the First World War. The SE5 A was a better gun-platform than the Camel and was said to be able to 'dive like a brick' – a useful attribute in days when many aircraft shed their wings if they dived too steeply. Flown by RFC aces such as Mannock and McCudden, it was also used by the US Air Service. This model shows a machine of A Flight, 84 Squadron, when commanded by Major W. Sholto-Douglas, later Marshal of the Royal Air Force Lord Douglas of Kirtleside.

17 Sopwith Dolphin by Tony Woollett (1:72 scale). An unusual design with the fuselage closely sandwiched between the upper and lower wings, the Dolphin had a reputation for being dangerous; no pilot liked sitting with his head thrust through the centre section of the upper wing, too close to the butts of the machine-guns for comfort. A bad landing could result in a serious injury or worse. This, plus experience gained in action, resulted in the removal of the upper Lewis gun mounting and the use of only the two Vickers guns in the nose. Some aircraft of No 87 Squadron had the Lewis guns remounted outboard on the lower wing. Large orders for the Dolphin II were placed by the French and American air forces, but none had become operational by the time of the Armistice in 1918. This model is of a Dolphin I flown by Captain F. I. Lord, C Flight, No 79 Squadron RFC, in July 1918.

18–19 Sopwith Pup by Michael Moore (1:160 scale). During 1917 the Pup served with both the RFC and the RNAS. It was said to be the most pleasant aircraft to fly built by Britain during the First World War. Armed with a single .303-inch machine-gun, the Pup was withdrawn from service as soon as the more heavily armed Camel became available. This amazingly detailed model depicts the first landing on a ship's flight-deck, when Squadron-Commander E. H. Dunning, RNAS, landed a Pup on the deck of the converted light battle-cruiser HMS *Furious*, 2nd August, 1917. This model has an incredibly small scale – perfect right down to the deck-landing crew, whose task it was to seize the aircraft when it came within reach and haul it down.

20 Sopwith Camel by Tony Woollet (1:72 scale). Perhaps the most successful fighting 'scout' of the First World War, the Camel was also notorious for being tricky to fly. It served with both the RFC and the RNAS, and was also used by the US Air Service. The Camel was either loved or feared by its pilots, but in the hands of a master it was a deadly weapon. This model shows a machine of B Flight, Naval Squadron 'Ten', 1917–1918.

21 Spad 13 by Norman Whitcomb (1:72 scale). An improvement on the already famous Spad 7, the Spad 13 was the most successful French fighter of the First World War and was flown by every Allied air force. It was flown by René Fonck, the top-scoring Allied ace, and by Major 'Eddie' Rickenbacker, the American ace. Like the Breguet 14 (*below*) the Spad 13 went to Poland and Czechoslovakia after the war, and was also flown by the Japanese. This model shows the machine flown by *Capitaine* A. Deullin, *Escadrille* SPA 73, in the summer of 1918.

22 Ansaldo SVA 5 by Donald Skinner (1:50 scale). Designed by Savoia and Verduzio and produced by Ansaldo, this was an excellent warplane of the First World War. It was originally intended to be a fighter, but was found to be so well adapted to the bomber and reconnaissance role that it was kept in service for over ten years after the end of the war. This model shows an SVA 5 on the Italian Front, 1918.

23 Breguet 14 by Tony Woollett (1:48 scale). This was one of the truly great airplanes produced by the First World War. The Breguet 14 first flew in 1916 and entered service in the following year. It remained in production (equipped with different engines) until 1926 and at least eight thousand of them were built. During the First World War the Breguet 14 was also flown by the US Air Service, and after the war by the Czech and Polish air forces. A special version, with a Rolls Royce Eagle engine, was built in Japan. During the 1920s the Breguet 14 made many famous long-distance flights. It was a two-seater bomber-reconnaissance machine with one fixed Vickers gun, two Lewis guns for the observer, and a bomb load of up to 520 lbs. This model shows a Breguet 14B 2 of *Escadrille* Br 127.

24 Fokker D VII by Norman Whitcomb (1:72 scale). This machine still ranks as one of the greatest fighters in the history of air warfare. It was ordered into large-scale production in early 1918, and in the course of the year it earned such a reputation that the victorious Allies marked it down in the Armistice terms as one of the specific items of German war equipment which had to be surrendered. By the Armistice more than one thousand had been produced, though not more than half of them had reached the *Jastas* – the German fighter squadrons – at the front. The D VII's great quality was that its performance did not fall off at altitudes where that of other airplanes became sluggish; the D VII was said to be able to 'hang on its propeller', even in a climb. This model shows the machine flown by *Oberleutnant* Karl Bolle, the last commanding officer of *Jasta* 2, in 1918.

25 Fokker D VIII by Norman Whitcomb (1:72 scale). Had the First World War continued into 1919 the Fokker D VIII would probably have surpassed its excellent predecessor, the D VII. It had a much better performance, although it was not so easy to fly as the D VII. Faulty wing construction delayed its full-scale production; when the trouble was corrected the D VIII began to arrive at the front in October 1918, but it came too late to see anything but limited war action. The D VIII represented by this model was flown by *Leutnant* Theo Osterkamp of the Imperial German Navy, who commanded Marine *Jasta* 2 and was the top-scoring German naval pilot of the First World War.

26

27

28

26 Handley Page 0/400 by A. M. L. Kennaugh (1:72 scale). A development of its predecessor the 0/100, this machine was one of the first heavy night bombers. These Handley Page bombers were big (100 foot wing span), strong (bomb load up to 2,000 lbs), and long-ranged (eight hours duration, and about 700 miles). By the end of the war the 0/400 was serving with seven RAF bomber squadrons, and the machine had made history in September 1918 when some forty 0/400s – the largest heavy bomber force seen up to that time – had attacked targets in the Saar. Far-sighted experiments in heavy bomb-load carrying were also made with the 0/400; the machine could carry the large 1,650-lb bomb.

27 Vickers Vimy by Tom Moore (1:72 scale). The Vimy was designed as a long-range heavy bomber capable of bombing Berlin. It is less well known that the Vimy was also intended to carry two torpedoes in an anti-submarine role, but the defeat of the U-boats made this unnecessary. Only three Vimys had entered RAF service by the end of the war, and the machine is best known for the long-distance flights it made after the war. This model shows the Vimy in which Alcock and Brown made the first non-stop air crossing of the Atlantic in 1919. The machine was specially converted, with extra petrol tanks fitted, to compete for the *Daily Mail*'s £10,000 prize. It was the third airplane to attempt the non-stop flight from Newfoundland; the first, a Hawker Atlantic, came down in the sea, and the second, a Martinsyde A, crashed on take-off. Alcock and Brown's Vimy landed in a bog at Clifden, County Galway, Ireland, after a flight of 16 hours 27 minutes over a distance of 1,890 miles. The actual machine can be seen in the Science Museum, London.

28 Vimy Commercial by Tony Woollett (1:72 scale). This was a civilian version of the Vimy bomber, produced with further long-distance flights in mind. This scratch-built model shows the prototype Vimy Commercial, G-EAAV, bought by *The Times* newspaper to attempt the flight from London to Cape Town. It got as far as Tabora, Tanganyika, where it crashed on take-off.

29 Westland Widgeon by Fred Henderson (1:48 scale). The first of these very popular two-seater light planes appeared in 1924. One point which made them liked by the private pilot was that their 'constant-braced' wings required no rigging – an important point in those days.

30 De Havilland Tiger Moth by Tony Woollett (1:72 scale). In many ways the epitome of private flying in the biplane age, the Tiger Moth was also the trainer in which most British pilots who fought in the Battle of Britain learned to fly. The RAF's basic trainer from 1933, the Tiger Moth was still in use with university and RAFVR flying schools in 1955. Over seven thousand were built, and the plane was sold to twenty-five different countries. Canadian Moths of the Empire Training Scheme had an enclosed cockpit because of the severity of winter conditions. Three hundred and eighty DH 82B Moths were produced as pilotless 'Queen Bee' target planes. After the Second World War many became private aircraft. This model shows a wartime Tiger Moth trainer.

31 Airco DH 4 by D. Warmington (1:72 scale). This famous and successful wartime bomber was put to many uses after the war, serving as a passenger and air mail carrier. It was in the latter capacity that the Liberty-engined DH 4 was used by the US Air Mail Service, one of its pilots being Charles Lindbergh. The DH 4 was also used in forestry patrol and fire-spotting.

32 De Havilland 88 Comet by B. Owen (1:72 scale). Three Comets took part in the 1934 England-to-Australia air race and one of them won: 'Grosvenor House', flown by C. W. A. Scott and T. C. Black. This model shows 'Black Magic', the Comet flown by the air record-breaker Jim Mollison and his wife, Amy Johnson. Engine damage forced the Mollisons to retire from the race.

33 Curtiss R3C Racer by W. R. Matthews (1:48 scale). In the 1925 Schneider Trophy Race there were three American entries, one from the US Army and two from the US Navy. All were Curtiss R3C1 landplanes fitted with floats. 'Jimmy' Doolittle, flying the same machine in which he had won that year's Pulitzer race, went on to win the Schneider Trophy while the two Navy planes failed to finish. Doolittle's plane was the last biplane to win the Schneider Trophy.

34 Supermarine S 6B by W. R. Matthews (1:48 scale). This was the plane that won the Schneider Trophy for Britain in 1931. Reginald Mitchell based the design on his successful S 6, giving it larger floats and the more powerful Rolls Royce 2,350 hp engine. Later in 1931 the S 6B raised the world air speed record to 407.5 mph – the first time that it had exceeded 400 mph.

35 Ford Tri-Motor by D. Warmington (1:72 scale). This plane was known as the 'Tin Goose'. With its all-metal construction, three engines, and spacious interior, it pioneered air transport all over the Americas. The 'Goose' had a crew of two and could carry twelve passengers. Among those who worked on its

design was James McDonnell, now President of the McDonnell-Douglas Corporation. This model depicts a scene from the early days of air transport.

36 A. N. F. LesMureaux by Fred Henderson (scale (1:72). Designed as a reconnaissance plane or fighter-bomber, these planes were supplied in small numbers to the French Air Force during the 1930s.

37 Fairey Flycatcher by A. M. L. Kennaugh (1:48 scale). The standard British Fleet Air Arm Fighter for over ten years, the Flycatcher was ideal for carrier flying and was a superb aerobatic machine. As well as its normal undercarriage the plane could be fitted with floats or amphibian landing gear. This is a Flycatcher of 405 Flight, based on HMS *Furious*.

38 Bristol Bulldog by Fred Henderson (1:48 scale). The Bulldog was one of the best aerobatic biplane fighters the RAF ever had. Small numbers also served with some of the Scandinavian air forces, as well as the RAAF and the RNZAF. This Bulldog is connected to a Hucks starter, which swung the propeller automatically.

39 Vickers Vulcan by Tony Woollett (1:36 scale). One of the first British planes designed specifically for passenger routes, the portly Vulcan – nicknamed the 'flying pig' – cannot be said to have been successful. Eventually nine were built, and were used by Instone Air Lines on the London-Brussels route. The Vulcan had a pilot-navigator and could carry six to eight passengers.

40 Short Scylla by Tony Woollett (1:72 scale). The Scylla was a landplane version of the Short Kent flying-boat, built to meet an emergency requirement of Imperial Airways. Only two of these planes were built: 'Scylla' and 'Syrinx'. The two airliners, which offered as much comfort as the famous HP 42s, remained in service with Imperial Airways from 1934 until they were taken over by the RAF in 1940.

41 De Havilland 84 Dragon by Tony Woollett (1:36 scale). The Dragon was ordered by Hillman Airways for its London-Paris service, and the prototype flew in 1932. It was an immediate success, and the demand for Dragons was so great that they were converted from six- to eight-seaters by the removal of the rear luggage compartment. Eight military Dragon 84Ms were delivered to Iran, armed with one fixed machine-gun and another for the observer. In 1933 the Dragon II was produced, with individual windows and a longer range.

42 Junkers Ju 52 by W. R. Matthews (1:87 scale). The European equivalent of the American DC 3 Dakota, more Ju 52s were produced before the Second World War than any other European airliner. During its career the Ju 52 served as a bomber, a troop carrier, a glider tug and a mine-disposal plane. In early 1971 there were still some sixty Ju 52s in operation in various parts of the world. This model shows a mid-1930s airliner of Deutsche Lufthansa; at one time over seventy-five per cent of the Lufthansa fleet consisted of Ju 52s.

43 Handley Page HP 42 'Heracles' by Donald Skinner (1:144 scale). Eight HP 42s had entered service with Imperial Airways by January 1932. Four were Es, for routes east of Suez, and four were Ws, for European routes. This is 'Heracles', a HP 42W, which had completed one million miles on European routes by 1937, and which reached the one and a half million mile mark before being wrecked in a gale in 1942.

44 'Spirit of St Louis' by W. R. Matthews (1:28 scale). This famous plane was flown by Charles Lindbergh on his solo flight from New York to Paris in May 1927 – 3,610 miles in 33½ hours. The plane, a specially-built Ryan NYP ('New York–Paris'), gave the pilot no direct forward vision; this was provided by a periscope, making take-off and landing somewhat hazardous. The plane was designed with one overriding purpose: to cram in sufficient fuel to enable it to make that one flight.

45 Handley Page Heyford by Fred Henderson (1:48 scale). This was the last heavy biplane bomber flown by the RAF. It had an unusually ungainly appearance; the upper wing was attached to the fuselage, to facilitate access to the bomb bay for servicing. The Heyford could carry 2,800 lbs of bombs and was armed with three Lewis guns. This is a Heyford Mark 1A of 'A' Flight, No 99 Squadron, in 1934.

46 Travel-Air 'Mystery Ship' by Fred Henderson (1:48 scale). This plane is typical of the designs produced between the wars for American air races. It had a definite influence on subsequent ideas for fighter design.

47 Hawker Audax by Tony Woollett (1:72 scale). Following the great success of the Hawker Hart day bomber, which when it first flew was faster than contemporary fighters, it was decided to adapt the design to other roles. The Audax was an army co-operation plane. It had one fixed machine-gun and a Lewis gun for the observer, and could carry 250 lbs of bombs. Several foreign governments ordered the Audax as a general duties machine, and different makes of engine were fitted to their choice. This model shows an Iranian Audax, powered by a Bristol Pegasus II radial engine. During the Anglo-Soviet occupation of Iran in 1941, some of these Audaxes were in action against the RAF.

48 Boeing P 26 by Fred Henderson (1:72 scale). One of the most distinctive fighters of the 1930s, the P 26 entered service with the USAAC in 1933. Known as the 'Peashooter', the P 26 was still in service with the Philippines air force when Japan invaded the islands in 1941. Its armament varied between two .30-inch machine-guns or one .30-inch and one .50-inch. This model shows a P 26A of the 34th Pursuit Squadron, USAAC, in 1935.

49 Boulton and Paul Overstrand by Harry Woodman (1:48 scale). The RAF ordered enough Boulton and Paul Sidestrands to equip one squadron. This medium bomber was remarkable for its versatility and manoeuvrability: it could be looped, spun, and flown on one engine. In the early 1930s a Sidestrand III was modified and fitted with the RAF's first power-operated turret. This prototype, originally called the Sidestrand V, became the Overstrand. It had a bomb load of 1,600 lbs and was armed with one Lewis gun in the power-operated turret, with one free Lewis gun in the dorsal and ventral positions. No 101 Squadron was the only RAF unit to be equipped with the Overstrand.

50

50 Hawker Fury II by Tony Woollett (1:48 scale). The most elegant of all the British biplane fighters of the 1930s, the Fury was also one of the most delightful to fly. It was amazingly manoeuvrable, and one of the highlights of the Hendon air displays was the sight of as many as fourteen Furies going through an impeccable aerobatics display tied together with rubber cord. The Fury was still in squadron service with RAF Fighter Command at the time of the Munich Crisis in September 1938, but had been superseded first by the Gladiator and later by the Hurricane by the outbreak of war one year later. Furies were supplied to many countries, sometimes fitted with radial engines. This model is one of three Furies supplied to Spain; the Fury, in fact, fought in the Spanish Civil War on both sides. With its cantilever undercarriage, this is one of the most attractive versions built; others had spatted wheels.

51

51 Gloster Gladiator by Harry Woodman (1:48 scale). The Gladiator was the last single-seat biplane fighter to serve with the RAF. It served in the gallant but futile Norwegian campaign of April 1940, operating from a frozen lake, having already been flown in the 'Winter War' of 1939–40 between Finland and Soviet Russia. Later the Gladiator saw action in the Western Desert; it was flown by Squadron-Leader 'Pat' Pattle, believed to be the top-scoring RAF pilot of the Second World War. Both in the Western Desert and in Greece, the Gladiator had many dog-fights with its Italian rival, the biplane CR 42 *Falco*. Gladiators were also flown by the Belgian, Swedish, Latvian, Portuguese, and Chinese air forces. This model shows a Gladiator Mk I of No 73 Squadron, RAF, in 1938.

52

52 Fairey Swordfish by Tony Woollett (1:48 scale). The famous 'Stringbag' was the only biplane to serve operationally throughout the European war. Designed as a 'TSR' (torpedo, spotter, reconnaissance) aircraft, it covered itself with glory in the raid on Taranto in November 1940 which neutralised the Italian battle fleet. Swordfish were used in the hunt for the *Bismarck* in May 1941 – the greatest air-sea pursuit in history – and their torpedoes crippled the German battleship, enabling the British Home Fleet to engage and sink it. Later they were used in the heroic attempt to stop the battle-cruisers *Scharnhorst* and *Gneisenau* from breaking through the Straits of Dover. The Swordfish probably did its best work in convoy protection, armed with depth-charges or rockets and flying from escort carriers. So successful was the Swordfish that it remained in service alongside its successor the Albacore, which was also a biplane design. When unloaded, the Swordfish had a maximum speed of 139 mph – but with its full load of 1,600 lbs of bombs, mines, or torpedoes, it was pitifully slow, and the German fighters covering the *Scharnhorst* and *Gneisenau* often found themselves obliged to attack the Swordfish with wheels and flaps down in order to get their speed down to that of the lumbering biplanes. The Swordfish had little in the way of defensive armament: one fixed and one free .303-inch machine-guns.

53–54 Boeing F4B and P 12 by D. Spicer (1:32 scale). When the name of Boeing is mentioned today, most people think of giant passenger jet airliners or jet bombers over Vietnam. When the firm first made its name between the world wars, however, it was with highly manoeuvrable little biplane fighters. The epitome of these, the F4 B (*top*), first flew in 1928. Initially the US Navy ordered twenty-nine as F4 B1s. This version had an uncowled engine. It was not long before the US Army ordered a batch as P 12s (*centre*). Later and larger orders were made for more sophisticated versions, and a total of 586 was finally reached – a high number for the inter-war period. The main foreign purchaser was Brazil, who ordered twenty-three. The F4 B shown here is a F4 B4 of Squadron VF-6, USS *Saratoga*. B4s served aboard the carrier until 1937. The P 12 is the commanding officer's aircraft of the 8th Pursuit Group, and is a P 12E.

55 Henschel Hs 123 by Donald Skinner (1:72 scale). Though it never served in large numbers the Henschel 123 earned a great reputation for its ability to take punishment and still get back to base. A ground-attack aircraft, it first entered service with the Luftwaffe in 1936, and in the following year some Henschels were sent to Spain to join the 'Condor Legion' fighting on the Nationalist side. Later all Henschels in Spain were handed over to the Nationalists, who used these aircraft until the late 1940s. When the Polish campaign began in September 1939 only one Luftwaffe *Gruppe* retained the Hs 123, but it was so successful during the campaign that it was kept in service until attrition finally ended its career in 1944. This model is of a Hs 123 A-1 of 8/*Schlachtgeschwader* 1 on the Russian Front, 1942.

53

54

55

56

57

58

56 Vickers Wellington by A. H. Butler (1:72 scale). On the outbreak of the Second World War in 1939 the Wellington was the best British bomber in service, and it remained the mainstay of Bomber Command until the large-scale arrival of the four-engined 'heavies' in 1941–42. It was remarkable for its basketwork 'geodetic' construction which enabled it to endure tremendous punishment and still keep flying. As well as flying day and night bombing raids, the Wellington was given minelaying duties and was fitted with a 'degaussing' ring to neutralise magnetic mines. Perhaps one of the most important functions of the Wellington was acting as a guinea-pig for the carrying of heavier and heavier bomb loads – it was the first aircraft to drop the 4,000-lb 'blockbuster' bomb. This is a Mark III, maximum bomb load 4,500; the later Mark X could carry up to 6,000 lbs of bombs.

57 Amiot 143 by Donald Skinner (1:72 scale). The Amiot 143 was the result of the French concept of the '*multi-place de combat*' airplane, similar to that of the American Flying Fortress: a bomber with no blind spots for its defending gunners, able to fight its way through to the target against all odds. The Amiot 143 entered service with the French Air Force in 1936 but was already obsolete by 1939, relegated to night bombing duties. During the 'Phoney War' (September 1939-May 1940) Amiot 143s flew reconnaissance missions and dropped leaflets over Germany and Czechoslovakia, the 143 being the only French machine with sufficient range for the latter task. After the short and brutal French campaign of May-June 1940 several 143s were taken over by the Luftwaffe, while a few were kept on by the Vichy French Air Force. In their latter capacity they were used as transports.

58 Dewoitine D 520 by Norman Whitcomb (1:72 scale). This was the best French fighter at the beginning of the Second World War. Unfortunately production did not begin until 1939, which meant that only a handful of these fighters were available when the Battle of France began in May 1940. The D 520 had an unusual wartime career. After the French surrender the Germans authorized continued production of the D 520, many of which joined Vichy French squadrons in Syria. When Germany overran southern France in 1942 many D 520s were seized by the Luftwaffe. Some were used as advanced fighter-trainers; some were handed over to the Italian Air Force; some fought on the Eastern Front with the Bulgarian and Rumanian air forces. In late 1944 the Free French forces managed to recover several surviving D 520s and turn them against the Germans retreating from France. About six hundred D 520s were built.

59–60 Heinkel He 111 by B. Owen (1:72 scale).
The He 111 was a mainstay of the German bomber
fleets during the Second World War. Supposedly
designed as a high-speed mail plane, the He 111
first flew in 1935, the year in which Hitler
proclaimed the official existence of the Luftwaffe.
In February 1937 some thirty He 111s were sent to
Spain to fight with the 'Condor Legion' on Franco's
side in the Civil War. Its high speed appeared to give
it immunity – an impression speedily corrected as
soon as it came up against modern fighter
opposition. The most obvious distinguishing feature
of the He 111 was its heavily glazed 'glasshouse'
nose. Over seven thousand of them were built, and a
Spanish version fitted with Rolls Royce Merlin
engines were still flying with the Spanish Air Force
in the 1960s. The machine shown here is a
He 111 H1, which had a redesigned cockpit. It served
with 9/KG 53 ('Legion Condor'), based at Lille,
during the Battle of Britain in 1940. As with other
German bombers, defensive armament was a weak
point with the He 111. It originally had three 7.9-mm
machine-guns, but this was increased to six;
sometimes one of the guns was a 20-mm cannon.

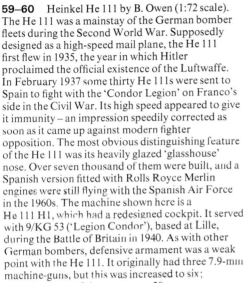

61 Reggiane Re 2000 *Falco* by A. H. Butler
(1:50 scale). A rival design to the Macchi C 200
Saetta (*see page 48*), the Re 2000 was not adopted by
the Italian Air Force. Instead it was produced for
export, being ordered by Sweden and Hungary.
This model shows a Re 2000 of No 1/1 Fighter
Squadron, Hungarian Independent Fighter Group,
on the Russian Front in the summer of 1942.

62 Junkers Ju 88 by A. H. Butler (1:72 scale). The
Ju 88 was one of the most amazing aircraft of the
Second World War. It entered Luftwaffe service in
1939, and was produced in greater numbers than
the combined total of all other German bombers of
the war. Over fifteen thousand Ju 88s were
produced, and about six thousand of them were
non-bomber versions. The Ju 88 served as an
orthodox level bomber, by day and night. It was
also a very formidable dive-bomber, and was much
used in anti-shipping strikes. It was used to lay
mines to drop torpedoes. High-flying Ju 88s were
used for photo-reconnaissance; low-flying Ju 88s
were used for ground attack and tank-busting, in the
latter role with a 75-mm Pak 40 cannon beneath the
fuselage. Fitted with radar, the Ju 88 became a
night fighter. It was used as an operational trainer –
and, most striking of all, as a flying bomb. As the
bottom half of a 'Mistel' composite a crewless Ju 88,
with an explosive warhead, would be steered to the
target by a 'pick-a-back' Messerschmitt 109 or Focke
Wulf 190 fighter which would separate once the
target had been lined up. The variant shown by this
model is a Ju 88 A4 (tropical version) of 8/LG 1,
Libya, 1942 – supporting the Afrika Korps.

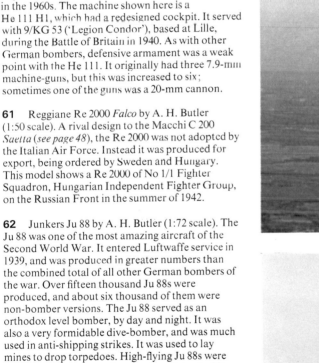

63 Avro Anson by Michael Moore (1:72 scale). The Anson was one of the great work-horses of RAF Training Command. This model shows an Anson Mark I of No 217 Squadron, RAF, with a Dutch aircrew.

64 Westland Lysander by Tom Moore (1:72 scale). The Lysander served throughout the Battle of France in 1940 as an army co-operation machine. Later marks were used for air-sea rescue, but it was most famous for its 'cloak-and-dagger' role, flying agents into occupied territory. This is a Lysander Mark I of No 2 Squadron, RAF, serving in France (1939–40).

65 Curtiss Hawk 75/P 36 by Gordon Stevens (1:72 scale). First flown in 1935, the Hawk 75 entered US service in 1937 as the P 36; some of them fought at Pearl Harbor. Another version was produced for export, most of them going to France; when France surrendered the survivors entered RAF service as Mohawks. This is a P 36A of the USAAC in 1939.

66 Potez 63 by A. M. L. Kennaugh (1:72 scale). This was the final development of a three-seat day and night fighter which first flew in 1936. It is a fighter reconnaissance version, the 63 11, with a glazed nose. This model shows a Free French Air Force Potez, serving with the Desert Air Force in support of 8th Army in 1941.

67 Douglas A 20 Boston (Havoc) by Michael Moore (1:72 scale). First ordered by France, the original A 20s intended for European use were diverted to Britain after the fall of France in 1940. These machines were mainly converted to night intruders, with heavier armament in the nose, and were named Havocs. This model shows a Boston Mark III of 88 Squadron.

68 Curtiss P 40 Warhawk and Messerschmitt Me 109F by Michael Moore (1:72 scale). The Warhawk was the mainstay of the USAAF in the first months after Pearl Harbor. Earlier marks had already seen service in the RAF as the Tomahawk and the Kittyhawk, as well as serving with the 'Flying Tigers' in China. This little diorama shows a P 40E Kittyhawk of No 112 Squadron, 239 Wing, Desert Air Force, making a pass over a shot-down Me 109F (tropical version). In many ways the 109F was the best of the Me 109 marks, but it was also thought under-armed with its single 20-mm cannon and twin 7.9-mm machine-guns.

69 Hawker Hurricane (*left*) and Supermarine Spitfire by B. Owen (both models 1:72 scale). The Battle of Britain was really the Hurricane's battle – over seventy-five per cent of all aircraft shot down between July and October were Hurricane 'kills'. This model depicts the plane flown by Sergeant-Pilot Josef František, the leading Czech ace, killed in the Battle.

70 Supermarine Spitfire XIV by Michael Moore (1:72 scale), in the act of 'tipping over' a V 1 flying bomb in 1944. The later marks of Spitfire were very different to those that fought in the Battle of Britain: much faster and harder-hitting, with cannon supplementing machine-guns.

71 Consolidated PBY Catalina by W. R. Matthews (1:78 scale). The Catalina first flew in 1935 and eventually reached the highest production total for any flying-boat anywhere. It was used early in the Second World War by RAF Coastal Command, and it was also built in Russia. After its distinguished war service the Catalina continued to operate for many years. This model shows the amphibious version, fitted with a tricycle undercarriage.

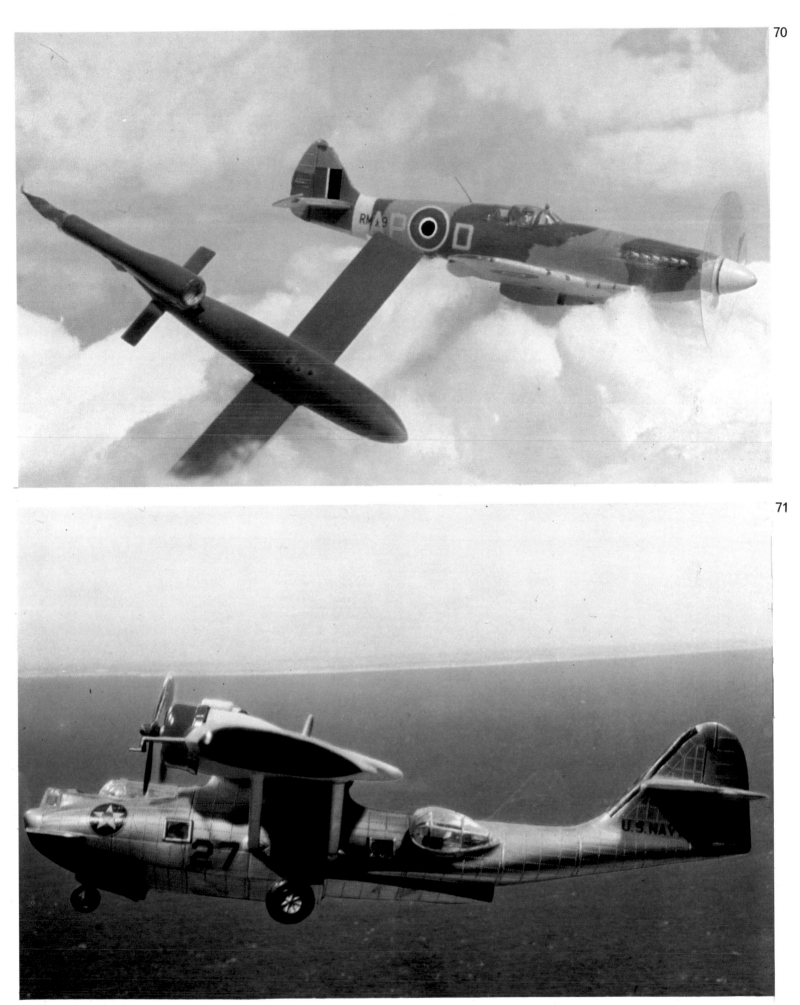

72–74 Junkers Ju 87 by Roger Chesneau (1:32 scale). The notorious 'Stuka' dive-bomber first flew in 1935, and by the outbreak of the Second World War had gone through many modifications to emerge as the Ju 87B. During the Polish campaign the aircraft became an integral part of the pattern of *Blitzkrieg*, making pinpoint bombing attacks on the enemy's rear areas and supporting the attacking German troops with hitherto incredible accuracy. Later in the war the Ju 87 proved that it was just as deadly against Allied shipping. But when faced with efficient fighter opposition, as happened in the Battle of Britain, the Ju 87 suffered heavily; it was slow, and its defensive rear armament was limited to a single 7.9-mm machine-gun. However, the considerable losses in the Battle of Britain did not result in a suspension of its production, and the Ju 87 was supplied to Italy, Bulgaria, Rumania and Hungary. Later – and especially in Russia – the Ju 87's ground-support duties were extended to include tank-busting, with twin 20-mm cannon. The Ju-87G packed an even heavier punch, with two 37-mm guns beneath the wings. The lower two views of Roger Chesneau's superb model show details of the engine and cockpit. This particular aircraft is a B2 flown by Hans Rudel with Stab III/*Stukageschwader* 2 – 'Immelmann' on the Russian front in 1941. Rudel became Germany's 'ace tank-buster', flying the Ju 87G, and was later credited with destroying 519 tanks. Armament for the B2 consisted of three machine-guns, two fixed and one free. The bomb load was one 1,102-lb bomb or one 552-lb bomb under the fuselage and two 110-lb bombs under each wing.

75 De Havilland DH 98 Mosquito by M. F. Harrop (1:48 scale). The Mosquito was one of the most versatile aircraft of the Second World War. Known as the 'Wooden Wonder' because of its all-wood construction, it was originally designed as a high-performance bomber which could out-fly any enemy fighter. But it proved so manoeuvrable that a fighter version was adopted with a deadly battery of four 20-mm cannon in the nose. There were fighter, bomber and photo-reconnaissance versions; the Mosquito was also the first British twin-engined aircraft to land on an aircraft-carrier, and Sea Mosquitoes were built for the Fleet Air Arm. No defensive armament was carried in the bomber version, which is shown by this model: a Mosquito BIV of No 105 Squadron, RAF.

76 Macchi C202 *Folgore* ('Lightning'). The *Folgore* was basically a C200 fitted with a Daimler-Benz engine, and it was probably the best all-round Italian fighter of the war. It served in North Africa, the Mediterranean, and Russia. This model shows a post-armistice plane which continued to fight with the Luftwaffe after Italy's surrender in 1943.

77 Polikarpov I 16 by Donald Skinner (1:72 scale), shown in pursuit of a Ju 87. This stocky little fighter entered service with the Red Air Force in 1934, armed with two rifle calibre machine-guns. The I 16 has the distinction of being the first monoplane fighter with a retractable undercarriage to be adopted by any air force. It served in the Spanish Civil War, flown by Republican pilots, where it earned its most famous nickname: *Rata*, or 'Rat'. Soviet pilots dubbed it *Ishak* – 'Donkey'. It was certainly an enduring beast; many thousands of all marks were produced, and the I 16 gave invaluable service when the Russian campaign began in June 1941. It soldiered on for many months before being replaced by much more modern fighters in 1943. This particular model shows a 'Type 24' I 16 as flown in 1941, with a maximum speed of 326 mph. Armament consisted of two 7.62-mm machine-guns and two 20-mm cannon; it could also carry six rockets.

78 North American P 51 Mustang by M. F. Harrop (1:48 scale). Considered by many to be the best American fighter of the war, the Mustang was most successful when fitted with a Packard-built Rolls Royce Merlin engine. A long-range fighter, the Mustang could fly to Berlin and back from bases in England. This is a Mustang III of the RAF, flown by Squadron Leader E. Horbaczewski.

79 Douglas C 47 Skytrain (Dakota) by Donald Skinner (1:72 scale). This was the maid-of-all-work of the Allied air transport services during the war. Many thousands were built and used in roles ranging from VIP transport to dropping paratroops and supplies.

80 Messerschmitt BF 109G by B. Owen (1:72 scale). The type of 109 which fought in the Battle of Britain was the E, soon supplanted by the F, the G, and finally the K. This is a Me 109G 5 bearing the markings of the *Gruppe Kommandeur*, 2nd *Gruppe*, JG-54 *'Grünherz'* in Russia, 1943.

81 Avro Lancaster by B. Owen (1:72 scale). This was the most famous British heavy bomber of the Second World War. The model is of 'G for George', flown by Wing Commander Guy Gibson in the dam-busting raid in May 1943.

82

83

82 Macchi C 200 *Saetta* ('Arrow') by Norman Whitcomb (1:72 scale). Designed by Mario Castoldi, the first *Saetta* had an enclosed cockpit, but later marks had an open one in deference to the wishes of the Italian pilots. It was not so fast as its contemporaries but it was very manoeuvrable and could take a lot of damage. It was later used as a fighter-bomber.

83 Savoia-Marchetti SM 79 *Sparviero* ('Hawk') by Donald Skinner (1:72 scale). The *Sparviero* was developed from a civil design which first flew in the mid 1930s. The bomber version came into service in 1937 and was used by the Italian squadrons supporting General Franco's forces in the Spanish Civil War. In 1939 it was decided to use the SM 79 as a torpedo-bomber, carrying two torpedoes. Both the torpedo and a bomber version were used by the Italians throughout the war. This model shows a SM 79 II, armed with its two external torpedoes.

84 Bristol Beaufighter by Michael Moore (1:72 scale). This famous RAF night fighter also served with the USAAF. It was designed as a private venture, using the wings and the rear fuselage of the Bristol Beaufort torpedo-bomber – hence the name. The Beaufighter came into service at the very end of 1940, fitted with the earliest form of air-interception radar, and soon scored many successes against the German night bombers. Later marks of Beaufighter, equipped with rockets and torpedoes, were used by Coastal Command against German shipping; and in the Far East theatre the Beaufighter was given the name 'Whispering Death' by the Japanese. This model shows a Mark IF of No 29 Squadron, RAF West Malling, Kent, in 1942 – the first RAF unit to receive the Beaufighter.

85 & 86 Westland Whirlwind by Tony Woollett (1:72 scale). The Whirlwind was produced in small numbers and equipped only two RAF squadrons, Nos 137 and 263. At low level it was the equal of any fighter in service, but unfortunately its Peregrine engines gave trouble; and as engine production came to concentrate on the Rolls Royce Merlin further development of the Whirlwind was halted. Whirlwinds were extremely successful in anti-shipping strikes and low-level strikes against coastal installations, with or without bombs.

87 Heinkel He 219 by B. Owen (1:72 scale). This was one of the few German designs conceived after the outbreak of war to see service. It was fortunate for the RAF night bombers that production of this outstanding night fighter was not given higher priority. Its development was hampered by indecision, but eventually small numbers reached the night fighter squadrons. The He 219 was armed with a 20-mm cannon in each wing; beneath the fuselage were two 20-mm and two 30-mm cannon. Most He 219s also had *'Schräge Musik'* cannon – two 30-mm guns in the fuselage, firing obliquely upwards.

88 Mitsubishi F1 M (code-name 'Pete') by Fred Henderson (1:50 scale). This Japanese naval spotter seaplane proved so versatile that it was used as a fighter, dive-bomber and convoy escort plane. It operated from cruisers, airplane tenders and island bases in the Pacific.

89 Mitsubishi A6 M *Reisen* ('Zero') by A. M. L. Kennaugh (1:32 scale). The Americans code-named it 'Zeke', but it will always be remembered as the notorious Zero, the most successful and feared Japanese fighter of the Pacific war. For two years it dominated the skies in the Pacific theatre until its heyday passed with the appearance of better protected and heavier-armed Allied fighters. However, the Zero stayed in service until the end of the war.

90 Grumman F4 F Wildcat by Michael Moore (1:72 scale). The Wildcat was the mainstay of the US Navy's fighter force during the early months of the Pacific war. It took part in the heroic but ill-fated defence of Wake Atoll – the only occasion when a Japanese seaborne invasion was repulsed – and in the battles of the Coral Sea and Midway. Later versions served until the end of the war, particularly aboard escort carriers. In British service the Wildcat was known as the Martlet. This is a F4 F3 of the US Navy, about 1942–43.

91 Kawanishi H6K (code-name 'Mavis') by Fred Henderson (1:72 scale). The Japanese had two fine long-range flying-boats in the H8K 'Emily' and the earlier Mavis. At the time of Pearl Harbor about seventy of the latter were being used for long-range reconnaissance duties, but lack of armour – a feature of most Japanese planes at the time – made them very vulnerable. They were later withdrawn and used as transports. The Mavis was armed with four 7.7-mm machine-guns and a 20-mm cannon. It could carry up to 3,527 lbs of bombs, or two torpedoes.

92 Hawker Typhoon by J. Chisman (1:48 scale). 'The most successful anti-tank gun' of the Allied armies in Normandy, the rocket-firing Typhoon did much to offset the Allied weaknesses in armour. With virtually complete Allied air supremacy and excellent ground-air liaison, German tanks could hardly make a move in daylight without being attacked by 'cab-ranks' of Typhoons. This is a Typhoon IB of No 198 Squadron, RAF, at the time of the battle of the Falaise Gap in 1944.

93

94

95

93 Chance Vought Corsair by M. F. Harrop (1:48 scale). When the Corsair entered service in early 1943 it was the most powerful naval fighter ever built. It soon proved its superiority over the Japanese Zero, and was a key weapon in establishing air supremacy in the Pacific theatre. The Corsair's ability to give close support to Army and Marine troops became legendary during the battle for Okinawa in 1945, and proved itself yet again during the Korean War. This is a Corsair of US Marine Squadron VMF-312, Korea, 1951.

94 Lockheed P 38 Lightning, by B. Owen (1:72 scale). The Lightning was a twin-engine, high-performance long range fighter and fighter-bomber. In this role it was extremely successful in the Pacific theatre, being flown by Major Richard I. Bong, the top-scoring American fighter pilot of the Second World War. The Lightning represented by this model was flown by Lieutenant C. R. Anderson, USAAF, of 443 Fighter Squadron, based on Boroka airstrip in Dutch New Guinea, 1944.

95 North American B 25 Mitchell, by K. Spackman (1:72 scale). The Mitchell was the first Allied aircraft to bomb Tokyo, when the 'Doolittle Raid', flying a special squadron of Mitchells, was flown off the carrier USS *Hornet* in April 1942. The Mitchell later served in all theatres of the Second World War, with the air forces of many countries. The aircraft shown here is a much later mark than that of the Mitchells which flew the 'Doolittle Raid' in 1942. It is a B 25H from the China/Burma/India theatre.

96 Nakajima Ki 84 *Hayate* ('Gale') by Donald Skinner (1:72 scale). Code-named 'Frank', this was a Japanese Army Air Force fighter of extremely high quality; it could out-climb and out-manoeuvre the American Mustang and Thunderbolt, although slightly slower than both. Heavily armed with twin cannon and machine-guns, the Frank also made an effective dive-bomber, carrying two underwing bombs. It entered service with the Army Air Force in the summer of 1942 and caused Allied fighter pilots much trouble.

97 Mitsubishi J2M *Raiden* ('Thunderbolt') by Donald Skinner (1:72 scale). Designed as a replacement for the famous Zero naval fighter the *Raiden* (code-named 'Jack') was plagued with teething troubles, but after these were overcome it became the best Japanese interceptor of the war. Armed with four cannon, it was used against the mass American B 29 Superfortress raids against the Japanese homeland. This picture shows a Jack belonging to the Naval Air Force, 1945.

98 Focke-Wulf Fw 190 by B. Owen (1:72 scale). The Fw 190 has been hailed by many as the best German fighter of the Second World War. This is a Fw 190D, wearing the black chevron of a *Gruppe* adjutant, Germany, 1945.

99 Boeing B 17 Fortress by B. Owen (1:72 scale). The legendary 'Fort' was the backbone of the US Air Force's bomber offensive against Germany. Its large number of defensive guns made it a formidable proposition for any fighter. This is the famous 'Memphis Belle'.

100 Consolidated B 24 Liberator by B. Owen (1:72 scale). The Liberator heavy bomber was produced in greater numbers than any other American aircraft in the Second World War. This is a B 24J of 457th Bombardment Group 15th Air Force in Italy.

101 Short Sunderland by W. R. Matthews (1:72 scale). Known to the Germans as the 'flying porcupine' because of its formidable defensive armament, the Sunderland flying-boat served with the RAF for twenty-one years.

102 Hawker Tempest V by B. Owen (1:72 scale). With its original design based on that of the temperamental Typhoon ground-attack fighter, the Tempest experienced many teething troubles during its emergence as a high-performance fighter. The only mark to serve during the Second World War was the Tempest V, with four cannon plus rockets and bombs, and a Napier Sabre liquid-cooled engine giving a maximum speed of 435 mph at 18,500 feet. The earlier mark, the Tempest II with a Bristol Centaurus radial engine, did not enter RAF service until 1946. The Tempest II also served with the Indian and Pakistani air forces after independence. This model shows the Tempest V flown by Pierre Clostermann in 1945 when he was commanding No 3 Squadron, RAF. By the end of the war Clostermann was acting as Wing Commander of No 122 Wing, while only holding the rank of *Sous-Lieutenant* in the French Air Force. Clostermann was the top-scoring French fighter pilot of the Second World War and his book 'The Big Show' is one of the best descriptions of the life of a Second World War fighter pilot ever written. In the closing months of the war, the Allied Tempest pilots had many opportunities to pit their skill against the flashing performance of the German Me 262 jet fighters, which remained a thorn in the side of the Allied air effort right until the end of the war in Europe.

103 Republic P 47 Thunderbolt, by M. F. Harrop (1:48 scale). Affectionately known as the 'Jug', the burly Thunderbolt was the heaviest single-seater aircraft to serve in any air force during World War II. Pilots were surprised by its ability to dog-fight with the far lighter fighters of the Luftwaffe, and the Thunderbolt was also popular because of its ability to sustain heavy damage and still get back to base. Thunderbolts were first used in the spring of 1943, over the Pas de Calais. Later, when it had been largely superseded as a long-range escort by the Mustang, the Thunderbolt was highly successful as a

ground-support fighter, supplementing its armament of four .5-inch machine-guns with bombs and rockets. This model is of a P 47M, a special mark supplied to the 56th Fighter Group – the top-scoring group of the US 8th Air Force. The 56th Group was the first to fly Thunderbolts and was the only one in 8th Air Force to keep them throughout the War. The P 47M had a maximum speed of 470 mph at 30,000 feet and was intended for use against the V 1 flying bomb. Engine trouble delayed its arrival, but it is credited with shooting down several Messerschmitt Me 262 jets.

104 Messerschmitt Me 262 by B. Owen (1:72 scale). The Me 262 was the world's first operational turbo-jet fighter. It has been called 'the plane that might have changed the course of the Second World War'. Over 1,400 Me 262s had been built by the end of the war in Europe in May 1945, but only about twenty-five per cent of them saw service – much to the relief of Allied pilots. The Me 262 fighter – known as the *Schwalbe* ('swallow') was ordered into full-scale production in May 1944, but this was delayed by serious factory damage caused by Allied air raids. In the meantime Hitler's obsessional search for a revenge 'Blitz Bomber' led him to order that the Me 262 must be pressed into service as a bomber – a role for which it was hardly suited. The result was the *Sturmvögel* ('Stormbird') variant, with its performance crippled by two 550-lb bombs carried beneath the forward fuselage. Later – but far too late – the fighter role was resumed with the aircraft's four 30-mm cannon supplemented with the devastating 'broadside' of twenty-four R4M 50-mm rockets – enough to blow a Flying Fortress out of the sky. Adolf Galland, the famous Luftwaffe ace and General of Fighters, said 'a Me 262 is worth more than five Me 109s'. The aircraft shown by this model was flown by *Oberstleutnant* Heinz Bär, Germany's top-scoring jet pilot.

105

106

107

105 Lockheed TriStar by K. Spackman (1:144 scale). The TriStar made the headlines when its production was held up by the Rolls Royce crisis, but deliveries to the airlines began in 1972. TriStar's design is ambitious: to carry up to 400 passengers at a cruising speed of 560 mph at 30,000 feet, with a range of 3,900 miles, powered by three Rolls Royce RB-211 22B engines. This model shows the second TriStar prototype in the livery of Eastern Airlines, which has ordered thirty-seven.

106 Boeing 707 by W. R. Matthews (1:125 scale). Developed as a private venture, the Boeing 707 was first ordered by Pan American in 1955. Since then over seven hundred of the various versions have been ordered, including some for Red China. One major improvement has been the replacement of the original engines with turbo-fans. This is a 707 320 of the Air France fleet.

107 Fokker F 27 Friendship by K. Spackman (1:72 scale). The Friendship is a short/medium range airliner which first flew in 1955 and is still in production. Powered by two Rolls Royce turbo-props, it can carry 36—56 passengers, and it has a range of 1,050 miles at a cruising speed of 291 mph. This model shows a licence-built Friendship by Fairchild-Hiller, in the livery of Bonanza Air Lines.

108 De Havilland DH 106 Comet by W. R. Matthews (1:144 scale). The first all-jet airliner, the Comet gave Britain the lead with a new form of air transport. But in 1954—55 came a series of air disasters and all Comets were grounded. One of the most detailed investigations in aviation history, including the use of underwater television to locate wreckage, tracked the cause of the trouble to a structural weakness in one of the windows. Later versions of the Comet have been extremely successful. This is the Mark III Comet, which was used for long-range development.

109 Boeing 727 by K. Spackman (1:144 scale). The 727 has beaten the record of its stable-mate, the 707 720, in the numbers of orders received over a shorter period. The prototype first flew in 1963 and by 1971 more than eight hundred and ninety had been ordered. Two special features have appealed to customers: a new system of wing high-lift devices which give the plane an outstanding take-off and landing performance; and speed of construction and delivery, much of the cabin construction being identical with that of the 707. The Boeing 727 has a range of 1,900 miles with 189 passengers. This is a 727 200 of Lufthansa.

110 North American RA 5C Vigilante by A. M. L. Kennaugh (1:72 scale). Originally designed as an attack bomber – the largest ever to operate from an aircraft-carrier – the Vigilante was later altered to the reconnaissance role. The first of these flew in 1962 and all original Vigilantes have been converted to the same role.

111 Northrop F5 Freedom Fighter by Fred Henderson (1:50 scale). Chosen for supply to friendly and Allied governments under the Military Assistance Program, the Freedom Fighter was first delivered to Iran in 1965. Since then at least twelve countries have been supplied with the F5A or F 5B. The B is a two-seater operational trainer version without the two fixed 20-mm cannon. Both versions have five weapon-attachment points and can carry a Sidewinder missile at each wing tip.

112 Republic RF84F Thunderflash by A. M. L. Kennaugh (1:72 scale). The Thunderflash is a special reconnaissance version of the F84F Thunderstreak, which in turn was a development of the P 84 Thunderjet. More than half of the seven hundred and fifteen built have been supplied to NATO countries. This is a RF84F of the Italian Air Force.

113 Lockheed YF 12A by W. R. Matthews (1:50 scale). This plane is believed to have been ordered as a U 2 replacement, but with a change of policy some of them were developed into air defence fighters. The main production batch, however, were SR 71As for long-range reconnaissance. This model shows the YF 12A, which is reported to have reached a height of 80,000 feet.

114 Mikoyan-Gurevich MiG 15 (*left*) and North American F 86 Sabre by A. M. L. Kennaugh (1:100 scale). When the MiG 15 was first encountered in Korea it was superior to any fighter in United Nations service. It eventually served in the air forces of at least fifteen Communist bloc countries. The Sabre was the 'answer' to the MiG 15, and was probably second only to the Phantom as an upholder of the Western alliance in the air. Thousands of Sabres were produced in the 1950s, and served in as many air forces as the MiG 15.

115 BAC (English Electric) Lightning by A. M. L. Kennaugh (1:72 scale). This was the first British production plane capable of reaching Mach 2 speeds. The Mark I entered service in 1960 and the Mark 6 in 1966. Originally the Lightning had two 30-mm Aden cannon as well as missiles; these were omitted in later marks, but they can still be fitted in a ventral pack.

117

118

116 North American F 100 Super Sabre by D. Spicer (1:72 scale). The Super Sabre made history as the first production plane capable of supersonic speed in level flight. It served with many NATO air forces as well as the USAAF during the 1960s. Powered by a Pratt and Whitney afterburning engine, it has a maximum speed of 864 mph at 35,000 feet. Its armament consists of four 20-mm cannon plus auxiliary weapons. This is a F 100D of the USAAF in Vietnam, where it was serving with 305 Tactical Fighter Squadron, 31 TF Wing, in 1965, before the adoption of the new battle camouflage.

117–118 McDonnell-Douglas F4 Phantom II – the most successful fighter used by the Western powers since the Second World War. It is in service with the USAAF and the US Navy, for which it was originally designed. The Phantom also serves with the RAF, the RNAS, the Royal Australian Air Force, as well as the German, Japanese, Iranian, and Israeli air forces. It is credited with the destruction of more MiG fighters than any other plane in Vietnam.

In the air: a Phantom F4K (117) of the British Fleet Air Arm, RNASY Yeovilton, by K. Spackman (1:72 scale). This is powered by two Rolls Royce afterburning turbo-fans and has a maximum speed of 1,386 mph. Armament consists of four Sparrow air-to-air missiles plus store points for the Vulcan 20-mm rotary cannon, 10,000 lbs of bombs, and other air-to-air/air-to-ground missiles.

On the ground: a Phantom F4F (118) by J. Ellis (1:48 scale) at Nellis Air Force Base, Nevada. This plane is armed with a 20-mm Vulcan rotary cannon, and it also has the latest miniaturised electronics. Its General Electric afterburning engine gives it a maximum speed of 1,584 mph.

119 Lockheed F 108 Starfighter by K. Spackman
(1:72 scale). Originally designed as a day interceptor,
the Starfighter was later supplied to NATO
countries as a tactical fighter. It has had a somewhat
unfortunate history in the new German Air Force –
there have been numerous fatalities – but the
Starfighter has been a great success in the Dutch,
Danish, Canadian, and Italian air forces. It has an
afterburning General Electric engine and a
maximum speed of 1,320 mph. Armament consists
of a Vulcan 20-mm internal rotary cannon plus
4,000 lbs of externally mounted weapons – two or
four Sidewinder missiles, a tactical nuclear
weapon, or rocket pods.

120 Grumman A6 Intruder by M. F. Harrop
(1:48 scale). The Intruder is a two-seat, low-level
strike fighter which was designed for the US Navy in
the light of experience gained in Korea. It has been
used in Vietnam by the US Navy and Marines, and
there is also an 'electronics counter-measures'
version fitted with sophisticated equipment for
jamming enemy radar. The Intruder has a maximum
speed of 685 mph at sea level and can carry up to
18,000 lbs of externally-mounted bombs, rockets
and gun pods.

121 Hawker Siddeley Harrier by B. Owen (1:72
scale). The Harrier is a development of the P 1127
Kestrel and was the first V/STOL (Vertical/Short
Take-Off and Landing) 'jump-jet' to enter service.
Fitted with a vectored thrust engine, it can take off
and land vertically, but normally uses a short run.
Such aircraft can be dispersed away from permanent
airfields and operate in close support of troops. The
Harrier equips several squadrons of the RAF, and a
version with a more powerful engine has been
bought by the US Marines as the AV 8A. This model
is of the Harrier GR Mark 1 of the RAF Conversion
Unit, Wittering, which took part in the *Daily Mail*
Trans-Atlantic Race in 1969, taking off from
downtown New York and landing in the centre of
London. The pilot, Squadron Leader Williams, took
5 hours 50 minutes to complete the journey from the
top of the Empire State Building to the top of the
Post Office Tower.

As the conquest of space begins, the airplane's ultimate form is being pursued: a transport craft capable of shuttling between an orbiting space station or space ship and the surface of the earth, and capable of surviving the searing temperatures created by re-entry into the earth's atmosphere. This problem of an earth-to-orbit ferry shuttle must be solved if the current system of a one-way 'splashdown' is to be improved upon. The machines shown by the models on this page reflect this exciting new phase in the continuing history of the airplane.

122 North American X 15 by W. R. Matthews (1:72 scale). Specially designed for research into flight at ultra-high speeds and great altitudes, the first X 15 was laid down in design studies in 1955. The early X 15s made many flights during the 1960s. They were taken up to high-altitude release points under the wings of Boeing B 52 Stratofortresses. When released, the X 15 pilot would ignite the rocket motor for the planned flight test, returning to the ground for a high-speed landing on the rocket's skids. These landings were made in desert areas. These spectacular X 15 flights, in which the piloted airplane reached the threshold of space, provided much invaluable knowledge.

123–124 The shape of things to come? These models by Barrie Armstrong (1:72 scale) depict two experimental re-entry vehicles: the M2 F2 and the Hl 10. In the search for a re-usable space shuttle, experiments have been carried out by the National Aeronautical and Space Administration authority (NASA). These experimental craft have rudders and elevons which give them far more control than their nickname 'flying stones' suggests. Like the X 15, they are carried to test height beneath the wings of B 52 Stratofortresses and released. They are powered by rocket motors, and have proved quite easy to control. The modified 'paper dart' shape has proved to be very promising in these tests. Other experiments have centered around tests with models in the 'heat tunnel', in which models are subjected to high temperatures similar to those caused by re-entry. One particular series of heat-tunnel experiments uses model nose cones made out of frozen oil to study the reactions of a streamlined body under these conditions. Even model meteors – plugs of nylon – have been used to study the effects of a meteor hitting a spacecraft in a vacuum! In all these tests and flying experiments, the model still plays a vital role today – just as it did for the Wright brothers and the other pioneers of the first airplanes.